INTUITIVE
STUDIES
A COMPLETE COURSE IN
MEDIUMSHIP

INTUITIVE STUDIES

A COMPLETE COURSE IN
MEDIUMSHIP

GORDON SMITH

HAY HOUSE

Australia • Canada • Hong Kong • India
South Africa • United Kingdom • United States

First published and distributed in the United Kingdom by:
Hay House UK Ltd, Astley House, 33 Notting Hill Gate, London W11 3JQ
Tel: +44 (0)20 3675 2450; Fax: +44 (0)20 3675 2451; www.hayhouse.co.uk

Published and distributed in the United States of America by:
Hay House Inc., PO Box 5100, Carlsbad, CA 92018-5100
Tel: (1) 760 431 7695 or (800) 654 5126
Fax: (1) 760 431 6948 or (800) 650 5115; www.hayhouse.com

Published and distributed in Australia by:
Hay House Australia Ltd, 18/36 Ralph St, Alexandria NSW 2015
Tel: (61) 2 9669 4299; Fax: (61) 2 9669 4144; www.hayhouse.com.au

Published and distributed in the Republic of South Africa by:
Hay House SA (Pty) Ltd, PO Box 990, Witkoppen 2068
info@hayhouse.co.za; www.hayhouse.co.za

Published and distributed in India by:
Hay House Publishers India, Muskaan Complex, Plot No.3, B-2,
Vasant Kunj, New Delhi 110 070
Tel: (91) 11 4176 1620; Fax: (91) 11 4176 1630; www.hayhouse.co.in

Distributed in Canada by:
Raincoast Books, 2440 Viking Way, Richmond, B.C. V6V 1N2
Tel: (1) 604 448 7100; Fax: (1) 604 270 7161; www.raincoast.com

Text © Gordon Smith, 2012

ISBN: 978-1-84850-836-1

Interior images: p.254 © Angela Nott; www.angelanott.com

Printed in Great Britain by TJ International, Padstow, Cornwall.

To all students on the spiritual path and especially to Steven for his inspiration

CONTENTS

INTRODUCTION

It wasn't long after the publication of my book *Developing Mediumship* that I began to get requests from people to run classes on the teachings in the book and give a more in-depth explanation of some of the exercises. It amazed me that people were becoming more interested in the teachings than the messages from the spirit world that I had become known for. I felt that giving people more of the teachings might be difficult, though, because I had done most of the teaching sessions during the course of a day or weekend seminar and I wasn't happy with that format. I knew that the development of mediumship could take many years.

For me, my circle, or development group, had always been important. It had been a part of my life since my early twenties and had been one of the things that had led me to dedicate my life to working as a medium. The development circle is where the medium really gains the energy and drive to work for spirit. Now, living in London away from the people I had spent every Sunday evening with for many years, all of a sudden I was aware of the distance between us. Though I knew we would always have a spiritual connection, I was missing the physical presence of my spiritual family. It had been a couple of years since I had actually been in a home circle and even though my life had been very busy and I had been doing more work than ever before, the lack of sitting regularly with a group of like-minded people had begun to affect me. I felt a sense of disconnection and a lack of the support that a circle can give.

I have felt for many years that when the spirit world needs me to do something, the opportunity will present itself before me. The need I had to be part of a development group again was becoming so persistent that I found it hard to ignore. So I knew it wouldn't be too long before the opportunity turned up.

Furthermore, there has been a purpose to each circle I have been in. I wondered what the purpose of this new circle would be. Somehow I knew it would involve more of the teachings.

1

MAKING CONTACT

*If you want to serve spirit, be sure to
know who you are serving first.*
Master Chi

It is strange how when we meet some people, we don't really understand what's happening at the time but somehow know that it has been an important meeting. This type of thing has happened to me many times and as I grow I learn to see what unfolds. This is what it was like one night around this time when I had just finished a demonstration of mediumship in a theatre in Margate, Kent.

I had got to the end of the book signing when two youngish guys approached me, one holding out one of my books to be signed, the other just standing at his side as if waiting for me to speak to him. Once I had signed the book I asked both of them if they had enjoyed the evening and if they were interested in developing mediumship. Neither gave the impression that they needed a message, so it felt natural to enquire as to their interest in the subject.

It turned out that both these young men were already involved in development, but were looking to learn more and find their way into a good circle. It made me smile when I asked their names and heard back 'Paul and Steven.' These are the names of my two sons and the young men were probably about the ages of my two sons at the time as well. Talk about feeling your age!

I found it a little funny that two 20-something men were presenting themselves to me for assistance on their spiritual paths. It's not the normal age range attending a demonstration of mediumship. But I was quite impressed that they were keen to learn, especially as I couldn't imagine my own boys wanting to develop with me. Then I suddenly remembered that I had been in my twenties when I first started on my path.

I guided both Paul and Steven to a friend of mine who, it turned out, lived not too far from them. Paul stayed in that circle, but Steven wanted to develop trance mediumship and felt that it wasn't really for him. He had already visited several circles and attended many one-day workshops and events to help him with what he felt was a natural gift of mediumship, but he hadn't yet found a circle where he felt safe enough to become himself. As he explained:

Even though I had some psychic experiences as a kid, I always thought that my life was as ordinary as those of the friends and family I grew up with in London. As a boy, I did all the things boys normally do, like play football and skip off school with my mates and use our lunch money to chip in for a packet of fags which we all shared down the local park.

As I got older, the local park became the local pub, where I shared stories about girls and football with my mates. I didn't have a clue about anything spiritual back then. Somehow, as you come through your teenage years into early adulthood, the only things that are important are what is happening at the time and you don't think beyond that.

I was working as a painter when I turned 20 and it was about a year later that I began to experience premonitions of future events; it was this that got me interested in the paranormal. At first the episodes were about my own life. For instance I had a premonition that I was going to meet a particular girl and walk home with her and she was going to tell me something personal about a mutual friend called Jay. At that particular moment a flock of pigeons was going to fly over our heads, a bit of brick was going to fall off the wall beside us and a bus was going to go past with Jay on it and she was going to say, 'Look, there's Jay!' However unlikely it might sound, two months later it all happened just as I had predicted.

After that I decided to try to predict something for my mum and my two sisters, because I thought they would be interested in that sort of thing. Actually, it wasn't a prediction as such, but one day I felt the presence of my nan around me and felt she was telling me to tell my mum that she had seen her taking out her wedding ring the previous evening. Apparently that had happened, and my mum hadn't taken my nan's ring out for about a year before that, so she was shocked by the information and began to take me seriously. She and my sisters encouraged me to continue with my new-found psychic gift.

At this point in my life I never shared what was happening to me with anyone other than my mum and sisters, though, because I felt that my mates and my dad would think I was crazy. To be honest, it wasn't the kind of subject that ever came up in the pub anyway, not unless it was used as a chat-up line on some girl.

It's strange looking back, because now I can see that the more I made a secret of my abilities, the stronger they became.

The first time I actually saw a spirit form was when I was 21. It is as clear to me today as it was back then. I just woke up in my room one night with a feeling of deep relaxation and calm moving over my entire body. I knew that when I opened my eyes there would be someone standing by my bed, and there was. It was a woman, and it could have been my nan, but I wasn't sure. I didn't really look at her face that closely. She was just standing there looking at me with a very calm expression.

Just at that moment my bedroom door began to open and I saw the figure of a man about to enter my room. He was about 40, but it all happened so quickly I don't really remember any more details about him. I just sat upright and called out 'No!' to him. I don't know why I did that. He didn't seem aggressive. I think I was just startled because it was the middle of the night. He didn't come into my room and the woman just vanished into thin air.

The amazing thing was that I felt no fear at all. In fact I just lay down and drifted off to sleep again without another thought about what had gone on.

The following day I went over in my mind what had happened and decided not to tell anybody for fear of ridicule. I had no idea what to do about it or where to get advice.

Several days later my sister came to tell me that she had been to see a psychic and the psychic had told her that she had a brother who had been visited by spirits. She went on to describe my feelings during the experience and the fact that I had called out 'No!' I knew then that I had to see this psychic for myself and try to find some answers.

When I saw her, she told me that I had psychic and mediumistic abilities and that they were now beginning to develop and that I should learn to meditate and try to be relaxed about what was happening. She gave me a book and a CD, which she said would help me learn some practices of meditation and also introduce me to my spirit guide. I had never heard this term before, but I was interested in finding out more.

Over the next three years I tried to meditate and I learned the practices of linking with my guide. But I wasn't really able to make much progress because I couldn't understand the feelings around me whenever I tried to communicate with spirit. All that happened was that I was becoming frustrated and confused. I felt isolated, too, because other than my sisters and my mum, I couldn't talk to anyone about it. I felt so cut off.

One morning I woke up feeling quite angry and thinking that if I had such a thing as a spirit guide, they should find a way of presenting themselves to me. Alone in my room, I called out, 'If I have a guide, then bloody guide me!' I even threw my trainer across the room in frustration. I felt very let down because I just felt that I was getting nowhere.

Three hour later my mother came home from shopping and dropped a newspaper on my lap, saying, 'Here, you're into all this stuff. I found it.'

*I looked at it and saw the title **Psychic News**. I was shocked when I opened it up and found a guide to all the Spiritualist churches in my area, and even adverts for courses on how to develop mediumship.*

When I asked my mum where she had found it, she told me that she had a pigeon-hole where she collected a monthly magazine for my niece and someone had put it in by mistake and she had only discovered it when she was nearly home. I wondered how much of a 'mistake' it had been. Within three hours of asking for help, there I was with answers and guidance.

*It was thanks to that **Psychic News** that I went on my first course of development. Soon afterwards I met Gordon. Destiny had delivered me to where I was supposed to be.*

Unfortunately, after much searching, I was running out of people who were holding the type of circle that Steven wanted to be in. He knew he had a gift – that first night in Margate he said to me, 'I'm going to be the bollocks at this!' – but he wasn't going to be easy to work with because once you got past that bravado, he was literally too shy to communicate. At that stage he would never initiate a conversation; I had to find ways of sensing what he needed in order to provoke him into a response. Most of the time he just hid behind the persona of a south London geezer, and that could be off-putting. And yet, underneath that tough exterior he was endearingly innocent and he really needed guidance. I realized that, rather than send him out to other people, it would be best to work with him myself. So I began to help him, together with Jim, my partner, who had sat in circle with me for almost 20 years. A new group was beginning to form…

Starting Out … Slowly

Remember, both teacher and student use the same book and share the same classroom. It's where they sit that defines them.
MASTER CHI

Even though I had run circles and taught mediumship for years, it was very different devoting all my efforts to one student, especially when that student had already been given many different ideas that were causing him to be confused about his gift. Though he had had experiences of both a psychic and spiritual nature in his life, Steven had never really known what to do about them or how to understand which was which. This was going to be a real challenge, I thought.

Instead of filling Steven's head with yet more new teachings, I decided to take him right back to the beginning and wipe his slate clean.

When you start out, you should never be in too much of a hurry to prove anything to others. Steven was anxious to prove everything, of course! It's natural to want to believe in what you are doing and to have others believe in your gift too, but very often this is where the rot sets in and you start to believe in things for the sake of it, things which are creations of your own mind rather than anything spiritual or psychic.

So the first thing I did was to teach Steven to sit in the silence and expect nothing. 'The silence' is what we term this particular form of meditative practice within Spiritualist circles. It is the foundation of our work, because it is when we know what it feels like to sit in a state of stillness, with no expectations, that we truly identify with ourselves on a mental level. I say it all the time when I'm teaching students, but you do need to get acquainted with your own mind and learn what it is capable of manifesting before you do anything else. It's all too easy to create thoughts which cause you to feel things, and before you know it you are talking about all sorts of visions and episodes which appear real to you yet are no more spiritual or psychic than the chair you are sitting on.

Steven wasn't expecting to start out this way:

When Gordon first taught me this exercise I was really surprised that he didn't want me to try to get a message or link to the spirit world. Up to this point I had been taught that I should try to see spirits in a clairvoyant way and get a message for the person or people I was sitting with. To be asked to sit still and not do anything was very strange. I must admit that

I couldn't see the point, but because Gordon was my new teacher, I decided to do the best I could. Now I think it was the most important lesson of my development, and without it I would never have grown.

Sitting in the silence is so important. It sounds easy, but if you have never tried to do it then you might find that your mind is a very busy, noisy place to be in. With practice and relaxation, however, it can become a powerful state of peace which can be your centre of control.

This is the one practice I always teach students first, because it is a form of meditation you can use anytime to find peace of mind or bring clarity to a situation. You don't have to be a medium to do it; anyone can do it. It doesn't make spirit come to you, but it will help you to begin your spiritual journey, which really does start with yourself.

EXERCISE: SITTING IN THE SILENCE

First, find a comfortable sitting position. Feel relaxed and calm. Make sure you do not feel restricted by tight, uncomfortable clothing.

Close your eyes.

Be aware of your posture. Try, to the best of your ability, to sit with a straight back. Allow your head to be as straight and steady as possible. If you feel it falling forward or to the side, try to imagine, if you will, a fine thread connecting to your crown and tugging you upwards.

Now breathe in through your nose, taking as much air as you can deep into your lungs. This relaxes the body and allows you to feel the first sense of peace.

As you breathe deeply into your body, become aware of your lungs filling with air, causing your stomach to swell, and as you breathe out, again from your nose, just relax and release the air from your body.

Start to become aware of your body's natural rhythm as you continue to breathe in and out. Feel the natural rhythm of breathing moving the body in and out.

Focus all your attention on the air which is being pulled into your body and then released.

Feel how focused and steady you have become with this simple exercise.

Be aware of the weight of your body.

And now visualize an abundance of pure white light sitting just above your crown.

Allow it to pour down through your head, deep down through your body, filling you with beautiful white light.

Become aware of how light your body feels, how bright.

Let the white light pour through your body in time to the rhythm of your breathing.

And feel the peace that it brings with it.

Become aware of how light and subtle you feel, as if you could move upwards, up and away from your body, into a higher part of your mind, the higher part where you find clarity as you realize that all is well.

And be at peace with yourself, recognizing that in this state of being you are still, you are peaceful and you are perfectly contented.

Allow yourself to send signals to your body from this higher state of mind, using that quiet inner voice which connects the lower and higher mind. Send positive signals of peace and contentment to your body.

Know that in this state of clarity you know no fear and that all the fears that your body has gathered and held can be dispelled.

Send down signals to your body that all is well and that you are exactly where you should be.

Be still, even though things around you are in motion.

Be calm in the face of all adversity.

Realize that you can tap into this higher state of self and that it is your right to do so at any time.

Take a little time to enjoy this elevated state of mind. Just sit in your own power in the silence of your mind. Be at one with yourself and recognize how good it feels.

And recognize that all around your body this beautiful brilliant white light is emanating in all directions.

Start to pull the light back into your body. Feel it regenerating and healing any old scars, any old memories. Shine the light into any dark corners where fear might be lurking in the body.

Feel the light flooding through your body and moving now in an upward direction and out through your crown.

Feel peace move through your body and begin to feel reconnected to the higher part of yourself that connects you to all things.

Feel how your body has accepted the relaxation.

And become more aware of your body, the weight of it in this relaxed state.

Start to breathe more deeply again, pulling air deep into your lungs, reconnecting your body and mind.

With each in-breath be more aware of your body and where you are sitting.

Take nice deep breaths. Draw oxygen into your body and bring clarity back to your mind. Bring yourself back to your waking state of consciousness.

And open your eyes.

Now you are ready to face the day.

. . . .

I would recommend that new students practise this exercise at least once a week on their own, and if they are part of a group or being taught by an individual, as was the case with Steven and me, it is a good exercise to use to start to build up a link of trust. This is how we build our own spiritual power.

Remember that in spiritual development you need to develop strength in yourself as well as a link to the spirit world. You need to prepare yourself to take responsibility for your life and your actions. Being mindful and relaxed does truly help you to see much more clearly what is appropriate and what is not.

The sense of being grounded is also one of the most important tools you can take on your spiritual path. Whenever I need to get a grasp on a confusing situation in my everyday life, I don't ask my guide to come and help me but instead use this meditation to get a sense of balance and calm before I make a move to change whatever is troubling me.

The first time I asked Steven to do this simple meditation, it had an amazing effect on him. Before this he thought that if he meditated, spirit would come and fill his head with images and messages and all sorts of thoughts. So he was surprised when I told him that the less he got, the better he would progress with his development.

This is what most students don't understand: they somehow assume that the spirit world has nothing better to do than fill our minds with messages, most of which make no real sense. Yet when we actually practise clearing our mind, chances are we might get clearer messages coming through when the time is right.

So I encouraged my new student to use this practice to clear his mind. It helped him to know that I still use it all these years down the line, either to get some clarity or to link with my guide, whichever is relevant.

I also told him that if he wanted to develop as a medium it would take him years and that if he didn't have the time to do it then he shouldn't bother continuing with our sessions. He was fine with that and quite happy to practise his meditation until the next lesson, whenever that would be. I knew at that point that he would grow in a spiritual way and that spirit would make itself known to him when he was ready.

There are many subtle energies around us which are actually our own life force and it is important to get to know them. When I started to practise meditation, I always got the sense that my body was gently vibrating. In the early days I thought I was having heart palpitations because the only thing I knew that sent out a rhythmic pulse was my heart. But now I know that what I was feeling was my own aura.

The aura is an energy which is part of us and emanates through us. It is difficult for most of us to detect because it is so subtle and vibrates at such a speed that it is normally beyond the reach of our five human senses. Some clairvoyants see it as a bright light surrounding a person's body. They may even see colours in it, which they can interpret to give information about the person's life. There is much to learn about this energy, but for me the first thing we need to do is to feel its presence as part of us.

Before we met, Steven had experienced what he thought was spirit communication but in actual fact was his own energy field opening up. He hadn't a clue that it was his own energy and had found it quite alarming:

Before I met Gordon, one of the things that most disturbed me was that whenever I thought a spirit was close to me I would feel that my heart was beating out of my chest. I must admit that it was quite frightening at times, because I thought my heart was really about to explode!

Not having anyone who could help me understand this sensation made me very concerned, but when I shared this with Gordon he was surprisingly calm and simply explained to me about the aura. Almost immediately the whole thing made sense and all my concerns just left me.

It had taken my teacher years to understand the energies he was working with, yet he helped me to understand them in minutes. I often think of all the people who are having psychic experiences and becoming afraid of them, as I did. Now I welcome the sensation, as it tells me that I am lifting my mind to a much higher vibration, from where I can link to the spirit world.

Teaching and Learning

I think it was around this time that I began to look at how much mediumship was changing. Mediums my age and older had practically all developed in circles, yet younger ones like my new student and other people who had recently embarked on this path were more used to workshops and quick, almost instant results.

I am not totally convinced by all the tricks and parlour games used today. For me, the teaching must be deeper. Teaching a student medium to read an object and pick up memories from it is one thing, but there is no sense of deeper spiritual understanding in such practices. Also, many of the quick-fix mediumship tricks can involve guesswork or encourage the student to fish for irrelevant information from the sitter, which I don't like. This lays down bad habits at the foundation of the training and I honestly don't allow this sort of thing into my training.

Getting Steven away from the type of teaching he had been used to was in fact very good for me too. It helped me highlight what people really needed in their development: good foundations, a simple understanding of the spirit world and how we interact with it and the reasons why we do it. It was time to get back to basics.

I made everything I did with Steven simple and easy to understand, and I created exercises which would demonstrate what I was trying to teach him and allow him to *feel* more of the spiritual essence rather than just receive yet more words. I didn't realize it at the time, but my new student was actually teaching me to become a better teacher.

All of the exercises in this book are those I used to help Steven progress step by step on his journey to realize his true gift.

Learning anything from the beginning can seem quite daunting at times. This is why in spiritual development I tell people that there isn't actually an end, as it were. Your practice will just become an everyday part of your life, which, if seen from the right perspective, is very positive and progressive.

No matter how much you think you know, or how far you think you have come on the spiritual path, there is always something to be gained by remembering the beginning of that journey. For me it was good to go back to the start and examine what I had learned, and I learned even more about it because to share it with a student so hungry to learn made it all so new again. There was something about teaching that brought me a whole new feeling of excitement.

Even though I have been in development circles for more than 20 years, and have developed skills as a medium and healer, I still enjoy the teachings I receive from the spirit world. I am still surprised and happy to call myself a student of spirit and I believe I always will be – to the end of this life and beyond. I also love sharing the teachings with others and giving them the pointers they need to further their own development. Understanding about spirit is exciting, even life-changing for many people. It certainly was for me, and this is why I feel compelled to share it with others.

The Calling Card

I knew that from the very first time I got Steven to sit in the silence that the spirit world was very close to him and truly wanted to work with him. I could see his spirit guide transfiguring his face when I sat and watched him. But I was determined not to give him too much too soon. His head was already full of archetypal images of what spirit guides should look like; the last thing he needed was more information. Now was the time to clear his mind and find a way to let him truly experience the spirit who was waiting to introduce himself.

Sitting in the silence over a period of time allows you to recognize your own thoughts and be aware of your body in a relaxed state. The idea behind this is to know yourself first, and then anything new which comes into your space will be felt and recognized at once. This is how we detect the presence of spirits around us. Each one will have its own calling card.

This is what happened to Steven:

I don't know how many times I sat with Gordon in the silence, but after a while the feeling that someone was standing beside me would just become so strong. I was also experiencing the same sensation each time – a tingling feeling around my face, always at the same point on my left cheek. Except for some thoughts which had no actual meaning to me, this is pretty much what happened each time Gordon and I sat together. And I always felt really good at the end of the session.

I had been told by a previous teacher that I had a North American spirit guide called Crazy Horse and after that I had been sure that I had seen this type of image in my mind when I meditated. But in my sittings with Gordon, whenever I asked about my guide all I got was this sensation on my face.

The first time I was instructed to ask my guide to come close and make himself known to me, the feeling on my face became so intense that I knew it was his way of letting me know he was with me. It was his calling card to me. And it was real – not like my Crazy Horse imaginings.

To get the calling card was all that Gordon had asked me to do during the sitting, and that is what I did. I didn't ask for anything else. But that was enough. It felt so real. And that sign became my first true interaction with my guide.

Building a connection with your spirit guide is so important on this path. You can believe what others tell you, or you can feel the reality of it by proper practice. Don't trust what your imagination offers. Seeing is not always believing, but in my experience feeling is.

EXERCISE: THE CALLING CARD

Take yourself into the silence, into your own quiet space, the space that brings you to the centre of yourself.

Just sit still and quiet in the white light that makes you aware of how still and contented you are.

At the most powerful and intense point of your meditation, send out a thought to your spirit guide – just one thought and no more. Ask if they will allow you to feel their presence in your space.

Wait for any change, any sensation or feeling that you might pick up. Ask no more questions. Do nothing other than register what change, if any, you are feeling.

Just sit in the presence of your guide and share the feeling of having them in your space for a moment.

Now ask them to step back.

Be aware if the feeling changes – be aware of your own atmosphere and if it has changed.

Start to breathe deeply into your lungs again.

Be more aware with each breath you take until you feel that you are ready to open your eyes.

Open your eyes.

Take a few minutes to slowly examine what you have just experienced. Look at it from a very calm position and ask yourself if you genuinely felt change around you, rather than saw things in your mind. Remember, this is about feeling presence, not seeing pictures.

. . . .

When you bring this practice into your meditation you must keep it as real as the practice of going into the silence. Don't invent spirit guides for the sake of it; be true to yourself. With each practice session you have, see whether the sensation that you feel is a calling card from your guide is always present and rule out anything that might normally cause such a sensation.

One woman I sat with in an open circle many years ago would often talk about the spirit breeze that she felt around her ankles each time spirit came to her. But she was sitting by a window at floor level which had a hole in the bottom corner next to her...

Like the lady with the draught around her ankles, I have identified what I thought was a spirit energy around me, only to realize later that it was quite normal and caused by something in the room I was sitting in. This was also a 'spirit' breeze that was actually coming through a broken window. Always try to apply common sense first, and only assume that the energy or experience is of a spiritual nature if everything else has been ruled out.

It is important to keep it simple at this stage and wait till you truly feel the presence of spirit. Believe me, you will know when it happens. That is all you are expected to do with this practice at this point.

Take it slowly. It took me years to truly get to know my spirit guide, Master Chi, and I know that much of what confused me was my own rush to know things. At first, every image that came to my mind, say of a Templar

Knight or a Native American, I assumed to be a picture of my guide, but they were all my imagination. The introduction to my real guide came through feelings – feeling his presence rather than seeing his image. After a while, I knew he was a small elderly gentleman. Then I went to see the medium Albert Best and he said, 'I'm not really supposed to tell you this sort of thing, but it's the right time to do it: your guide is an Oriental gentleman.' Then the next day I saw my psychic artist friend Dronma and she drew him. And the very next night my teacher Mrs Primrose said, 'I'm going to have to tell you this because your guide wants me to,' and she gave a description of the same person. For me, it was great to get three confirmations in such a short space of time.

Steven demonstrated a patience that I never had. He also had the luxury of not having to make the mistakes that I had made. I was determined not to allow my student to create false messages or phenomena. Gradually, over a period of about two years, he not only got his guide's calling card but also a sense of his body. At different times, he felt his presence as both a young and an old man. The calling card became more pronounced, and at one point Steven felt as though he'd actually had a stroke down the left side of his face. He started to sense his guide's personality too. He felt that he was a much more balanced person than he was: an awesome presence something like the Dalai Lama. Once, he saw him as a scribe sitting at a desk writing and thought he looked quite well to do. He asked if he could know his name and heard it come back as Chen Tsung, but he never told anyone. Then later, when I was in trance, my guide confirmed it to him.

Raising the Vibration

Your guide is always close by your side, and though you may not be able to recognize this at first, in time and with practice and patience, you will. The moment we send out our thoughts to our spirit guides and ask them to let us know them or to give us a calling card that we can identify them by, there is a quickening in our own energy. There has to be an acceleration which can heighten our senses, otherwise we can't link with the spirit world.

This is because our world and the spirit world can never truly be open to each other unless there is a change of vibration in one of the worlds. That was something my guide shared with our group during a rare channelling session. He informed us that either spirits had to down their rate of vibration in order to become dense enough to be felt by us, or we had to raise ours in order for them to have an effect on our energy field.

One of the exercises I was given by my guide to help Steven to develop was to let Steven come close enough to me to feel my energy and how it changed as my spirit guide came closer. This gave him the chance to experience a much more heightened energy.

I think this is a good experiment for students to practise with each other. It allows a student to get a sense of what is happening around a medium when their spirit guide is working through them. Being close to heightened energy like this will also naturally bring the student's vibration to a much higher state.

The exercise needs to have two people working together and another instructing them, so we called upon Jim to take us through it.

EXERCISE: RAISING THE VIBRATION

One person sits in a chair in front of another person, who stands with their hands resting gently on their partner's shoulders.

The student who is sitting goes into the silence and is still.

The student who is standing then lifts their hands just an inch or so from their partner's shoulders and tries to sense the aura which surrounds them.

The aura can become tangible if the student is open to sensing it at this level.

The person leading the exercise asks: 'Are you sensing any change of temperature, any hot or cold spots, any vibration or pulsing at this point? Just try to be aware of any new sensations around your partner.'

The person sitting asks their spirit guide to come into their space. As this is happening, it will change the vibration which surrounds them.

The person leading the exercise then asks the standing student, 'Is there an immediate change in the aura or is it subtle? Be aware of the energy and allow your mind to open up to it. Try to notice any changes in your partner's auric field. Can you actually sense the presence of their guide, or maybe even the calling card they use?'

Now the student sitting asks their guide to step back and thanks them for their presence.

The student standing takes deep breaths and relaxes as they allow their hands to drift back onto the shoulders of their partner.

The person leading the exercise asks them both to come back to full focus and share their experiences.

. . . .

It is good for people to share their experiences in an exercise like this, because it does help them to link together, which is important if they ultimately want to start a circle to work more deeply with each other. This exercise also helps people to bring each other's vibration up to a higher level and to become more synchronized, which is also useful as it is just as important for all the people in a circle to be open and in tune with one another as it is for them to be in synch with spirit.

It was so good to do this exercise with Steven and I also got to sense how he handled the energy, what he was feeling and where to take him next in our sessions.

The practices I had been doing with my student were getting him ready to feel spirit in the way he had first told me he wanted to. Spirit was always ready to work with him, but he needed to be fine-tuned, if you like, to realize the reality of his spirit guide and to receive the lessons for his life.

One of the things I was finding with my new student was that he was being prepared to sit in a proper development circle.

2

THE CIRCLE

*When people come together and dedicate
goodwill towards others yet ask for nothing
in return, they open the way to love.*
MASTER CHI

My first development circle was in Mrs Primrose's church in Glasgow and was an open circle, which meant that it was open to everyone. So of course people would drift in and out because they were curious, or would visit us twice or three times but find it wasn't for them. Usually there would be about 40 people each week, all at different levels of development, but even with all the comings and goings there were at least 12 people who always came and were the core which built the energy in the group. I think back to that circle and see that watching what my teacher did was preparation for what I am doing now.

There were times when I would ask Mrs Primrose if we could start a private circle with just the core of the open group, because there would be such a lot of power for spirit to work with then, but she always told me that where I was now was right for me and that the time would come when 'the spirit would move me'. She was right, as usual – sitting in a large open circle meant that I experienced many different people, all with different ideas about spiritual development, from the very humble to the greatest egomaniacs that were out there. This type of experience has been so valuable to me in the work that I do today. Being able to understand where people are in their development is vital when you are teaching.

Not everyone who came to our circle wanted to be a medium or healer; some came to investigate the subject, some came because they were lonely, or sad and needed comfort, and some were just downright deluded and saw it as a place to show people how important they were.

My teacher kept me in this class for seven years, and I do see why. It allowed me to learn about people and their needs and requirements, and also to work out what I could do to help when there was a genuine talent who was a bit lost on their path. That was one thing my teacher often asked of me in the last year of my development with her. She would point to someone and say, 'Go find a way to that one.' Once, when I asked her why we kept allowing a man into the circle who was loud and disruptive and dominated many of our sitters, she simply told me that all energy could be used by the spirit world and they would refine this man's energy if we allowed him to stay.

After her passing, Jim and I started our own private circle with five other people who had sat with us in the open group. The spirit *had* moved me and it felt the right time to build our own circle.

I had come to learn that when spirit needs you to do something, everything starts to fall into place. A certain type of synchronicity occurs that just confirms your very thoughts. This certainly happened with the private circle. I was demonstrating mediumship so much at that time that I never had much time to go to the church, but I was missing my development. I asked Jim if we should start our own circle and if so, who he thought would be right to sit with us. I had already made a list in my mind, but I wanted to see if we were thinking along the same lines.

Jim came up with exactly the same people that I had in mind and I wondered if they had been getting the same impressions themselves. This can happen when you go into a circle – out of nowhere you get a thought or a feeling about contacting a person and you have no idea why, but they are thinking the same.

In fact I didn't even have to ask the first sitter, Sandra – she called me and asked if I would be interested in starting a circle with her and Christine, who just happened to be next on my list. Apparently they had met the day before and both had an insistent feeling of being in a circle again and had seen Jim and me there.

I also had a strange dream at this time about a friend of mine who had never sat in a development circle and, as far as I knew, had never wanted to. Dronma was a Tibetan Buddhist and although she had an interest in spiritual subjects – I always thought she was a wee bit psychic – she had never given the impression that she would like to be part of a Spiritualist circle for developing mediumship.

But then, just as we were preparing to start our new circle, Dronma called me to say that she had had a bizarre dream which had involved her sitting in a circle of people all linking hands and that she felt she had to find out about it.

The short version of the story is that she became our fifth member, and the fact that she was an artist was great for the group because we all thought that she might be able to draw the images and symbols our spirit guides gave to the circle.

Within a week we were seven in number. The other two were Margaret, an older lady who was a customer of mine in the hairdressing salon and was eager to be in a circle, and Pat, a working medium who had approached me and asked if I was thinking of starting a circle because he felt he needed to do some more development to help his mediumship.

All this came about from sending one little thought out into the universe, as it were. Our circle was now complete.

For the next seven years we would meet every Sunday night at eight o'clock at our flat and open up our sacred space. Over the years, so many wonderful connections were formed. The most obvious was the bond of true friendship between us. I think we all learned from one another and whenever one of us had a problem, the rest of the group would be there to help in a flash.

An amazing energy built up in that circle and we received so much concrete evidence from the spirit world and some very clear teachings from our spirit guides. Master Chi would come regularly in the early days of the circle and give instructions which would help us build the circle. Other teachers would speak at times through some of the other sitters, often giving us advice on our everyday lives and the problems we were facing.

There was never a shortage of spiritual guidance in the group and there was definitely always a sense that the circle was working on a much deeper level than the open circle we had experienced before. And the drawings that Dronma would do during the circle were great confirmation of what each sitter was tuning in to when they were connected to spirit.

Even away from the circle there was a common telepathy working between us – one person only had to be anxious or in need and everyone would become aware of it and report in. Even though it has been almost ten years since we ended the circle, the network of sensitivity that was built between us still exists.

I believe that just as the open circle was preparation for the public mediumship and teaching work that I would do later, that first private circle taught me the mechanics involved in development which I was now using to teach Steven.

Preparing for the Circle

Steven sat with us for a year and a half as our student before we actually opened ourselves to working as a circle. I knew that he would feel different working in a circle and that the power he and I had got used to building between us would change because of the addition of Jim, so I started to bring Jim into our training sessions from time to time to allow Steven to feel the change. Jim and I were used to sitting in circle together, but I also wanted Steven to feel part of things. Any new person in a circle brings a new energy with them and can take time to settle in. Many students I had met had told me that they had been invited into a circle but had felt uncomfortable as they had never really felt a part of things. I wasn't going to let that happen to Steven. I had prepared him carefully, and even though he still had a lot to learn, by the time he started sitting in circle with us he was somewhat in tune with both Jim and me and had the ability to let spirit get close to him.

We decided to sit in our flat on a Sunday evening at seven o'clock. This was the day we had sat in our previous circle in Scotland, so it felt natural for us. I think it is important to have your circle in the same place at the same time each week, because it helps to build the energy in that place and also fosters a kind of dedication and devotion to the special time set aside for the spirit world.

By now our new member quite understood what he would do during the session. He had learned to clear space in his mind and to raise his vibrations to allow his guide to come and sit in his space. So all that was left to do was the practice.

Many people assume that spirits will manifest and all sorts of phenomena will occur when we sit in a spiritual circle. If only they knew the energy and years of dedication it would take to create such a thing! All we wanted to achieve with our circle was to create a sacred space where we could gather and ask our spirit guides to join us. From the beginning we told Steven that we would dedicate whatever energies built in the circle to someone we knew, or had heard about, who needed some help. This is the nature of a circle: to help others worse off than we are.

So, as in his earlier lessons, all Steven had to do was be still and let go.

EXERCISE: SITTING IN CIRCLE

Choose the seats you wish to sit in and get yourself comfortable.

Join together in holding hands to open up the session and take a moment to become aware of one another's presence.

The leader of the circle will open with a short prayer to the spirit world offering the circle as a place for spiritual work to be done during the sitting.

Release your hands and allow them to fall comfortably onto your lap.

Take yourself into your own silence and start to become aware of your own power.

Sit in your own power and be aware of the vibration around and through your body.

Be comfortable in this state of mind. This is something you should now welcome into your space.

When you feel ready to reach out to your spirit guide, ask them to come into your space and let you feel their calling card.

When you feel the acknowledgement that your guide is with you, welcome them to sit with you so that you can become more accustomed to their energetic vibration.

There will come a point when the spirit guide will recede and step away from you or, if you feel that you are satisfied with what you have experienced, you can ask them to direct the energy you have built between you to those who need it more.

After this, begin to focus on your body more and on the room where you are sitting as you draw deeper breaths into your body.

When you feel ready, open your eyes and wait for all other sitters to be fully back with you.

Join hands and allow one of the sitters or the group leader to close the circle by thanking the spirit world.

Share your experiences and see if there were any common feelings.

· ·

Any small group of people of like mind who are interested in forming a circle can use this exercise. Please don't expect too much to happen in the very early days, as it really does take time to build energy as a group to allow spirit to work with you. Just enjoy the experience of sharing this space with each other – that is the most important thing to accomplish at the beginning. Enjoy the experience of sitting with friends in a calm and peaceful place where you can all relax and build a link between you. If you put in the practice and dedication, in time the spiritual energy will get stronger.

Both Jim and I were willing to be very patient with Steven. Yet we both felt very comfortable, even in the early sessions, and already there was an amazing sense of power building. Somehow it felt different from the past episodes, but it was far too early to know where this circle was going.

Our student, however, seemed to develop very quickly. I remember thinking it was like seeing someone grow from childhood into adulthood. After only six months of weekly sittings he was beginning to understand more of the reasons why the spirit world wishes to work with us and teach us – his whole take on things was changing and he was beginning to flourish:

Even before I met Gordon, I wanted to sit in his circle. But on my first few attempts to do so, even though he had already taught me many things through meditation and late-night conversations about the spirit world and so on, I couldn't actually take in what was happening.

I could certainly feel my mind becoming calm and clear, and the presence of my spirit guide felt even stronger than before, but I always had the feeling that I should be getting something or doing something else. As hard as I tried to stay still and clear, I couldn't help but go on little journeys back into events which had happened to me in the past. At first I didn't understand why, but at the end of each circle we would discuss what was going on and what we had felt or experienced, and it felt natural to tell Jim and Gordon about the episodes of my life that had come up for me. Both of them would listen and then, rather than give me an answer, would ask me to find the answer for them.

After I had given my explanation of what I felt was happening, if I was correct, Gordon would just say, 'Good.' If he felt I was skipping over things, he would say nothing but give me a look which said I wasn't trying hard enough.

I know that this might sound a bit selfish, but now I know why this was happening to me and not the others, and I do feel that it is an important part of early development to understand it. Now I know that in the early circles I was being shown emotional things which I would have to look at and sort out in myself before I could move on to the next level, as it were. It made sense, because I kept asking my guide to teach me to grow, but how could I? There were so many things in my mind that I had to clear out first. This, I was told, was my responsibility.

Once again it was a lesson in patience. And I didn't realize that even at this stage we were still really at the beginning.

My intention at this point was not to make my student a medium – only he and spirit could do that – but simply to get him ready for spirit to bring him his lessons. All I had really done up to then was take someone who had potential and bring them up to a standard to start the process properly. Even when you have an awareness of spirit, you still have to prepare yourself as a vehicle, or channel, for spirit to work through. Part of this process is meeting yourself and facing your fears and doubts. This is where Steven found himself at this point. But the speed with which he was moving forward was heartening.

Not only did my student benefit from our Sunday meetings, but I began to feel a renewed sense of connection with my spirit friends. Even though I was often giving messages to people as a medium, experiencing spirit in a circle is so much more powerful and rewarding when you stay with it and take your time.

The other thing that had happened was that Jim and I were now back in circle, which we had both missed – after all, we had been doing this for most of our adult lives. Two years away from the spiritual classroom had been enough. It felt good to be back, and more than this, there was something developing in me which I felt strongly would show itself in the coming circles.

3

HEALING

Healing is to make better and bring balance.
'How do we do this?' you ask.
Compassion is the answer.
Even saying the word makes me feel better.
MASTER CHI

A year after starting our small home circle, we were all just so happy to be a part of it. It was like being tuned in to a power that made you seem safe and protected from the everyday problems that everyone has to endure in this physical life. There was an amazing sense of wellbeing that brought healing which left you feeling nurtured and balanced.

Even though our little group was just three in number, the force between us was strong because we never tried to take from the energy build-up. Instead we just asked to give and be a part of it.

So many circles begin with thoughts like, 'What can we get from this?' or 'What will it do for me?' or, worst of all, 'How long will it be before we get some kind of phenomena?' Not with us, though. We were all very content to just sit in the silence and feel the presence of our spirit guides in our space. Two of us had been here before and the new guy had been very well prepared for this.

Sitting in this type of spirit energy makes you develop whether you want to or not. Steven was recognizing many things about himself that he needed to face and overcome, and now he felt that he was connected to a higher force which gave him the confidence to do this. A lot of healing was taking place, and not just in our student – both Jim and I also experienced the healing of emotions which we realized had been stored very deep in our psyches.

I think we all accepted that our circle at this point was all about healing. Even when we felt that spirit wanted us to learn a lesson, it was always about healing.

This seems to be a very natural progression in spiritual development. Healing is the core of development and a great tool to have as a medium. It is one thing to give a message to someone as a medium, but if it lacks compassion and depth, and there is no intention to heal, it is merely words.

When I went into my original circle, first of all Mrs Primrose allowed me to sit and unlearn all the things I thought I knew about mediumship. And only after three years, when she knew that I was truly feeling the spirit world around me and my need to rush and impress people was gone, did she take me on to the next step, which was healing.

I was confused at first. I somehow imagined that it would be better for me to work on mediumship. It felt more natural to me to give messages to people, and even though I hadn't been fully trained as a medium, it was where I always saw my development going. But my teacher knew best, so I went along with it and every Tuesday night I worked with a trained healer who guided me in the art of spiritual healing.

It was the right thing for me because the very nature of healing appealed to me right away. And the first thing I was taught in the healing group was to let my healing guide come through.

The Healing Guide

I had become used to Chi connecting with me in the circle and it had never dawned on me that it wouldn't be him who would be working through me on the healing. However, just after I had understood who Chi was, I had become aware of a Tibetan man there as well. His presence became more apparent when Mrs Primrose asked me to practise healing. She obviously knew that he was my healing guide waiting to come forward.

Learning to recognize the change of spirits working with you isn't that difficult, because once you have got to know your spirit guide's calling card, and how it feels when they come into your space, when you feel a completely different essence bringing a new set of sensations and a completely different calling card, it is easy to recognize the change.

I have met so many people who claim that they have dozens of spirit guides from all different planes of existence. They might have, but I don't really see the purpose of this myself. To learn about a guide and get used to their familiar signs keeps us from becoming confused. It is when we are used to these signs that we are ready to expand our awareness to accept another spiritual teacher who wishes to add a gift like healing to our energy. This is also less confusing than a mass of spirit guides.

There are people who don't feel a different guide or essence for healing, and that is fine too. It seems to me that the way I've been taught by spirit, with a spirit guide and a healing guide, has been so that I can learn to differentiate between the guide who works with me when I give messages or philosophy and the healing essence when I perform hands-on healing. When I feel the healing guide it makes it clear that the person in front of me needs healing rather than a message. It is my signal.

There has to be a reason why spirits come to us, and therefore it makes sense for them to teach us to sense them slowly and understand who they are and why they are there. And this will only truly happen when we show them that we are ready to take the next step.

For students who are familiar with their spirit guide and feel that they wish to share the spiritual energy they have been building and use it for healing, here is an exercise to help take that next step:

EXERCISE: MEETING YOUR HEALING GUIDE

As ever, sit and relax and breathe deeply to begin.

Follow your practice of going into the silence and building the power.

Sit in your own power and be aware of how you feel in this heightened state of self.

When you feel that your awareness has expanded enough, ask your guide to come into your space.

Feel the calling card that you have now become so familiar with and say, 'Welcome, friend.'

Sit for a while in the presence of your guide and just let your energies blend together.

Enjoy spending some time sitting in this spiritual energy field.

Now ask your guide to step out of your space and notice how you feel in the absence of their energy.

Ask them to step back into your energy and again feel the union between you.

Now ask if you have a healing guide and if you are ready to meet them.

Try to sense if there is any response to your question; use your heightened senses to feel the response.

If you feel at this point that the response is positive, ask if you can meet your healing guide. Ask if you might be allowed to sense their calling card or receive a sign that they are connected to you.

Be aware of any changes which happen when your healing guide comes into your space.

Just as when you were meeting your guide, take some time to feel your healing guide's presence and be comfortable in their energy.

When it feels right, ask your healing guide to step out of your space and thank them for allowing you the experience of sitting with them.

Thank your spirit guide and ask them to step back, again with thanks.

Relax and begin to breathe deeply into your lungs, filling them with air.

Still breathing deeply, with each breath you pull into your body, come back to where you are.

Become more focused on the room and when you feel ready, open your eyes.

. . . .

Like me, at first Steven was a bit bewildered when he was told to ask his healing guide to come and introduce himself. Like me, he had just got used to the guide he had come to know and now there was another to learn about.

It was actually in our circle that he met his healing guide first. One of the reasons we started to train him as a healer was because I would look at him from across the room at the end of our circle and often see his healing guide transfiguring his face. The guide was a young Chinese man with a dark moustache and high cheekbones and the most piercing dark brown eyes. It was dramatic to see, particularly because Steven's eyes are light blue. I can still never totally get used to that – talking to a person and seeing a spirit starting to build over their face. I'm hearing a person talk to me but seeing the face of someone else – how bizarre!

But this is always my sign now with my students that something is changing with their work, and for Steven, his healing guide was showing himself to me so that I could direct Steven towards healing.

Performing Healing

I sat in the healing group for almost two years before I progressed on to mediumship, and in no time at all I was allowed to work with a trained healer on some of the patients. At first the healer would choose a person who wanted healing and sit them down, then place her hands on their shoulders. I was asked to stand at the front and ask my healing guide to come and give energy to the proceedings. And that is what Jim and I did with our student.

Jim had been practising spiritual healing for over 20 years and was the best person to take Steven through some of the simple but fundamental practices of healing work. He had learned his own craft before he met me, when he was part of a charismatic group in a Catholic church where the priest was very unorthodox and got together a group of people who shared his belief in the healing powers of the Holy Spirit.

Jim took to healing like anyone who was naturally compassionate, and soon wanted to learn more about the subject and others who were using it. This was one of the reasons why he found himself in Mrs Primrose's church: to investigate the way healing was practised and taught.

Mrs Primrose bonded with Jim very quickly and she was glad that he wanted to stay and learn more about the healing work that was happening in her church. More than that, she instinctively knew that he was a natural healer and that whether it was the Holy Spirit or his own spirit healing guide, power would channel through him to help others.

Jim and I began to have sessions of healing in our own private circle and we wanted to teach people to understand the mechanics of what happened when a person was channelling healing energy. For instance, were there times when the person gave healing energy from themselves, and if so, did that have a different effect on either patient or healer, or did healing energy always come from a higher source than the channel? There were exercises that would test our spirit helpers and allow us to get answers during our sessions. We learned that sometimes the spirit world would choose not to heal someone at a certain time and the healer would then take it on themselves to channel their own positive wishes as a separate force. This could benefit the patient, but the healer would very often feel tired afterwards, which wasn't the case when the healing energy came from a higher source.

One of the most obvious discoveries for us back then was that we would always work with our hands on the patient's physical body when the problem was physical, but when there was a mental or emotional problem we found that our hands were guided to work out in the patient's aura.

Jim also ran a healing clinic in the Glasgow Spiritualist church for several years, where up-and-coming healers would practise on the church members. Jim would give them good guidance on healing, working with their healing guide and being sensitive to the patient's needs. Having spent much of his life working in hospitals as a nurse, and also as a carer with people with special needs, he was probably the right person to serve the spirit world as a healer. It was for this reason that I knew he would be ideal to work with Steven on the next course of his development.

At the beginning, Jim only allowed Steven to practise healing on him. Then sometimes, when I was around, he would ask him to work on me. The main idea at this point was just to give him instructions on how to begin and end the practice, and where he should stand in relation to the patient, and so on.

Jim would give Steven exercises in tuning in and feeling for current ailments, or scars from past illnesses, to see if he had the kind of instinct that would allow him to actually feel a person's pain or discomfort, and whether he had other skills which would help him, for example seeing the part of the body affected by illness.

All of this practice was really beneficial to our student because it opened him up to learning more about healing and about empathy. This was so important to his overall development.

The way Steven took to his healing work and began to bond with Jim was impressive. Even away from the healing, they would sometimes meet when I was working abroad and spend time talking about their lives. It was so good for Steven to learn to trust other people and begin to volunteer information about his life and his intention to become a healer or a medium. He was becoming comfortable enough to let down some of his barriers and start to heal episodes and memories from his own life.

Jim gave Steven a simple practice to do on his own, which was to heal himself once a week. We had both learned from Mrs Primrose that if you wish to heal others, you should first heal yourself. It is important to recognize your own level of pain in this life. I have often felt that we can only heal others as deeply as we have been healed ourselves, and that if we have experienced pain, it is easier to identify it in others.

Jim would ask Steven to sit in the silence and invite his own healing guide to come and help him find areas of his past that needed to be understood and healed. For instance, he would ask for the most immediate problem to be shown to him, whether it was a problem of the body or mind, and with the help of his healing guide he would identify it and begin to heal it. When sitting in the silence we can lift our mind to a higher perspective and see solutions which are not always obvious in everyday life, when our mind is cluttered with so many things.

Jim was a very good healer and had given hundreds of healing sessions in his lifetime, but working with Steven allowed him to enjoy the teaching side of his work again. Seeing that his student was so enthusiastic and keen to learn was inspiring.

Jim recognized that Steven was quite like me in that he was a natural healer, but his ability to see and feel during his practice meant that he could go on to practise mediumship if he wished. But the most important thing about the sessions they had together was that Steven was gaining confidence and awareness. He wasn't confused by the images coming into his mind, as he had been before. Now he had the intention to heal and a far more developed sense of empathy. So he was bringing something very different to his development.

We started bringing people who had asked for healing to our flat and letting Steven work on them with Jim. It was interesting to see how they reacted to the energy they felt when both healer and student gave energy to them.

All of us who serve the spirit world are instruments used to channel energy from the higher, more subtle spiritual realms into this physical world. Whether it's a message from a loved one or healing in some form, the role of the person giving it is to be as clear as possible, so that whatever is coming through is as pure as possible. This is one of the teachings I was given by my guide many years ago and when I serve spirit in any capacity, my aim is to be as clear a channel as I can. I find that if my mind gets in the way, or I try to think about what I'm doing, then the message or healing will be blocked.

This is why I like to teach people as I was taught, by great teachers on Earth and in the spirit world, to allow our healing guide to get as close to us and fill as much of our space as they can. By now Steven was beginning to trust more in his healing work and was definitely at the stage where his healing guide would overshadow him and control his hands:

Many times in my development circle with Jim and Gordon I would feel an impression to move my hands, but I always resisted this and kept them on my lap. When my connection with my healing guide became stronger, though, it became harder not to go with the impression.

It felt as though there was a great build-up of energy around my hands. This energy acted like a magnet, pulling at my hands so strongly that I eventually had to let go and allow them to rise off my lap and into the air. The feeling was amazing because no matter how much I tried, I couldn't control the direction this magnetic energy was taking my hands in.

It felt as though my arms had become lighter also, and that all the bones and tendons were being manipulated by another mind. I felt overwhelmed, as I had been sitting in the circle for the past few years with my eyes closed waiting for something to happen, and now there was this!

Not long after this I had an even better experience when the spirit energy just lifted me onto my feet and I found myself standing up in the middle of the circle with my eyes closed. I was trying to be sceptical, but it was hard to doubt when my hand just shot forward and I felt that my fingertip was touching another.

The same force meant that I couldn't open my eyes and see what was happening, but my finger started to move as if following the other person's finger. This all happened at such a speed that I had no time to think. That was the strangest feeling – that my hand was being manipulated by my guide's mind and he was demonstrating the most amazing coordination without being able to see through my eyes.

In time, I have come to understand that this was done in order to teach me to trust spirit. So now, whenever I work with my healing guide, I let him move my hands because I trust that he knows much more than I do about what needs to be done with the patient. The episodes in the circle were my guide's way of preparing me to allow spirit more use of my body. I now see that it was all down to trust.

Working as a healer, or even practising under the guidance of a trained healer, means that you have to trust more in the spirit you have been learning to link with in the earlier practices. It is also a time when you have to learn to use your intuition and instinct more.

Much of what I learned at this stage of my own development was to feel the conditions the patient was carrying – their pains, or sometimes the weight of their emotions, and so on. These sensations often come to you when you are working as a medium too, only then it is the spirit on the other side who is transferring them to you to make clear how they passed away, or how they suffered before their passing. Much of what I now feel when I'm working as a medium comes from what I learned working in close contact with patients during my early sessions of healing. Again it brings it home to me that Mrs Primrose knew exactly what she was doing with me, and now, as a teacher, I realize how my students benefit from practising healing, both early on and later in their development.

4

GERMANY

*Travel is good for you, it gives you the chance
to connect with others and learn of their ways.
To learn and become interconnected
is the way of spirit.*
MASTER CHI

Around this time I was travelling in Europe, working as a medium and giving talks on the spirit world, spiritual healing and all things life after death. Whilst in Frankfurt, in Germany, I was asked if I would give a workshop on how to develop mediumship. It would run over a weekend for about 40 students, all at different levels and with different interests in the above-mentioned subjects, and I agreed to do it.

Because it was such short notice I had no actual plan to follow, but I had done this kind of thing a thousand times before and thought I would be spontaneous and let spirit guide me.

Normally that is never a problem for me, but that day I found that somehow people didn't seem to get the idea. I had a group of 40 people sitting in a circle and I was trying to give a kind of general teaching about development which featured snippets from years of practice, but I soon learned that there was such a difference in what the people in the room understood about the subject that I was losing the attention of most of them. Some didn't know what a medium did, others asked me how many spirit guides they might connect with during the course of the weekend (which just made me smile!) and yet others took great delight in emphasizing that they had taken a week-long course at a psychic college, where they had learned to become trance mediums and now felt they needed advanced teachings.

It was at this point that I realized what all of them really needed. I gave a very serious talk on the length of time it took to develop as a medium and the responsibility that went with it. I informed them that this might be a weekend workshop, but if any of them were genuinely interested, I would take them back to the very beginning and give them some proper methods to try. Then we would see who would like to know more after that.

There was complete silence in the room when I finished speaking. Even the 'great trance mediums' looked sheepish. And even they stayed to see what I was going to teach them.

What *was* I going to teach them? When I began to talk to them about meditation, once again I found out that most of them had done some form of it, but again the forms were weird and wonderful, and none of the students had truly understood what they had learned, or what to do with the practice. So I began to outline the first four exercises I had taught my young student back home: 'Sitting in the Silence', 'The Calling Card', 'Raising the Vibration' and 'Sitting in Circle'. When I told the group how well Steven had done in just a couple of years, I certainly got their attention. They could relate to the confusion he had felt when he had first come to me, and they loved the fact that I had organized a training system which followed a more regimented order of exercises. More than this, they wanted to learn more about them.

I found that the weekend's programme was turning into a breakdown of the work I was doing back home. Interestingly, it seemed to be much more accepted than some of the previous workshops I had done where students were led in a guided meditation through the countryside to a lake or pond, then taught how to give a message and read each other's aura, and so on and so forth. This was the way short day or weekend workshops were being taught, but I had never been very comfortable doing this type of workshop. When I worked for different Spiritualist organizations, I would rather take the students who had already been in a development circle and allow them to just sit and learn to link with the spirit world or, if I was allowed to, I would give a talk on the subject. It always made me feel uneasy asking people I had never met to try and give messages; I hadn't been taught like this, and I wouldn't expect other people to learn that much from this type of exercise. If anything, this form of teaching just confuses people because it seems so instant and isn't at all like the proper system, which takes years.

Now it dawned on me that even though I only had a short time to teach these people, I would rather give them practices that they could take home with them and use to much better effect than the quick-fix development of before.

The weekend was such a success that many of the students wanted me to go back and teach them more about development in this structured way. They wanted me to construct a proper course which would run for a year or so and would allow them to do work at home and build circles where they could learn to work more deeply with spirit. Some even asked me if I would bring Steven along so they could ask him what it was like to start from the beginning and truly find a link with your spirit guide.

The organizer of the event kept at me for weeks after I'd gone home, asking if I had thought about running this type of course. In fact, word had spread and there were so many students waiting to join that I could have just stayed there and taught for the next three years.

So, with all that in mind, I began to break down the development I had come through over the years that I had sat with spirit. I also tried some exercises out on Steven that could be useful to the students in Germany.

I had almost a full year to turn the teachings into modules which could be undertaken over five weekends throughout the following year. This would mean that between each module the students would have time to practise what had been taught. In development, people need time to process what they have experienced in circle, or in this case in class, before moving on to something else. It's all very ethereal and needs time to filter through you until you understand it.

As I had done with Steven, I asked all the new students to start by sitting in the silence. It is so important to clear your mind. When people first do this they may experience symbolic visions or sense emotions which have been locked away inside them for years. It is easy to assume that these are messages from the spirit world which have deep meaning if you can work them out. This is where you need to have a teacher who understands this, and is not given to fanciful thinking themselves. So I asked the students to keep notes of what happened each time they sat with others or on their own and tell me when they had an experience which they could not explain, or thought was from spirit, and I would help them to comprehend the meaning.

All Steven's spirit messages seemed to be turning into pieces of his life which needed to be addressed and I expected the same to happen with the other students. It is only once we get the rubbish out of our minds that we can truly begin to develop.

Sensing Emotions in Others

The next exercise I wanted to work on with Steven was how to sense emotions in other people. I had found this to be such a useful experience in my own development. As a medium it is essential that you can feel the emotions of the people you are trying to help, and understand how best to work with them. Obviously a medium will depend on the spirit world to pass the message through from the loved one on the other side, but the medium should develop sensitivity towards the person sitting in front of them.

The following is a similar exercise to the healing practice in that it should be worked with two people, one sitting and the other standing behind them. The difference here is that we are not trying to sense spiritual energy, but human emotion.

EXERCISE: SENSING EMOTIONS
· ·

Students who are standing, clear your mind and prepare your breathing.

Now, resting your hands on your partner's shoulders, just relax and breathe away any thoughts or frustrations from your mind.

Allow your mind to go into the silence which you now know so well and be still.

Be aware of the fact that you are standing behind someone, resting your hands on their shoulders.

Try to feel this person through your hands. How do you feel in their energy? Does it make you contented, or is there any feeling of unrest? Make a mental note if you are aware of anything different from what you were initially feeling.

Be still in the state of peace you have created and allow it to pass through you and into your partner through your hands.

Students who are sitting, recall now an emotional event which was life-changing for you. Try to relive this for a moment, to bring back the feelings and see and hear in your mind what actually happened.

And now let it go; allow the memory to drift away from you and take your mind into a peaceful state through the breathing technique which you have become accustomed to using, and just relax.

Students who are standing, register anything you felt when your partner was doing this. Make a note of anything that occurred, whether it was felt, seen or heard in your mind. Just keep those memories as you also relax.

Now, both of you, with each breath come back to a waking state and recognize exactly where you are as you open your eyes.

Sit facing each other. The one who was standing, describe how you were affected (if at all) by the emotional change in your partner.

The one who was sitting, talk about the emotional event you recalled and see if there is any connection between what you brought back to your mind and what you were told by your partner.

. . . .

Remember, this is not a reading. This exercise is about how to sense human emotion, that's all. I would never encourage students at this point to try to understand why they felt certain changes, or work out how to correct them. To begin with, just being aware of them is enough.

The first time I got Steven to take part in this exercise, he wasn't even aware that he was picking up my emotional memory!

I had never been asked to do this type of exercise before. When I had been asked to tune in to someone on a workshop or course in the past it had always been to try and get a message for them from the spirit world. It was strange just to try and read a person. I didn't feel totally sure about what I was doing. But I did as Gordon asked me, put my hands on his shoulders and cleared my mind.

I felt very connected to him through my hands. I felt a heat in them. I just kept calm and remembered not to think about anything that my mind might throw up, but instead let my body be used to receive any kind of emotional change.

But then I assumed that I wasn't doing it right because suddenly my stomach was turning and I felt nervous. I couldn't help also feeling excited, but maybe frightened too, and then I stopped trying to feel anything at all and opened my eyes.

When Gordon asked what I had felt during the session, I said I hadn't really got anything. I thought I needed to see pictures in my mind, so I didn't think I'd picked up anything at all. Gordon made me close my eyes and told me to go back in my mind and remember anything I had told myself when my eyes were closed, so I did, and I repeated it all to him. He just smiled, because he'd been remembering when one of his sons was born and how nervous he had been, yet excited and frightened at the same time.

Now, having used this technique many times, I have a much better sense of how to distinguish the feelings of people around me if I tune in to them.

One of the important things about this practice is that it helps the developing medium to have empathy with a person. Some of the students who have used it have felt a sadness and immediately found that they could relate to it in their own life; others have experienced a depth of emotion coming from their partner that they couldn't possibly understand, but were nevertheless moved to help them.

Steven's first attempt showed me that most of the students we would be using this on would also be likely

5

THE CLASS

It is amazing what lies beyond the
little field of belief that you live in.
The fence which surrounds it is fear.
Take down the barrier of fear and
expand into what is real.
What is real can only be found beyond belief.
MASTER CHI

Steven, Jim and I tried out many exercises over the following months and the day was approaching when I would take the new lessons back to Frankfurt.

I decided it was time for my student to learn to pass on the knowledge he had learned, and I felt that it would do him good to teach some of the exercises to the students. After all, it was not that long since he had learned them himself, and he was having great success practising them. It seemed to me that his enthusiasm would rub off on others.

Steven, however, had other ideas:

A week before we travelled to Germany, Gordon told me that I would teach some of the exercises and I was terrified. I never thought that I could do it, nor did I want to.

I knew that Steven was very nervous about talking to people about his interest in mediumship, but I also knew that he would have to lose that fear if he was going to progress and work as a medium. So it did him no good to protest. All I did was remind him of what my old teacher said whenever I said I wasn't ready to do something: 'Tough.'

The First Module

On the opening morning of the first module we had 40 eager students sitting in front of us. Well, maybe five or six eager students – the rest looked as though they were about to be tortured. Come to think of it, so did Steven at my side. Bless! However, they had all signed up for this and now it was time to put things into action.

For me, it would be exciting to see how our new group would take to our teachings, though I knew it would also be difficult to concentrate with a very disgruntled student beside me telling me he wouldn't do this or say that and that he wasn't ready for this. Just one of the joys of becoming the teacher, I decided.

After an opening talk in which I explained how patience and practice would determine how well the students would proceed, we got going.

The morning was taken up with the first exercise about sitting in the silence. I believe in the old proverb, 'When the student is ready, the teacher will appear.' But I also have learned that the student must make themselves ready, and that, I feel, is what we do when we clear our mind and create a space for spirit to come and teach us.

It was quite amazing how many of the group appreciated this, and many questions were asked. I let my student answer those:

Q: How long should we sit when we do this ourselves?

Steven: *I sat for somewhere between a half-hour and 40 minutes to begin with, though there were times when I just fell asleep. I found that when I tried to sit every day this would be when I would be most likely to fall asleep, so I stuck to twice a week for half an hour each time. Now I sit once a week for one hour and I find I can manage that fine. I always try to sit in the same place at the same time wherever possible, because it helps me to build the energy in that room.*

Q: Should we do it every day or several times a day? If we do it more, will we proceed more quickly?

Steven: I used to believe that if I sat more often, I would learn more and in a shorter time, but now I know that you can only learn what you are supposed to at any given time. Also, leaving time between sittings makes you look forward to it more and you benefit more. Things happen in your life that you have to deal with, but if you know you have something each week which will give you space, then it's worth keeping to that system; it kind of makes it special.

Q: What happens if a thought gets into my head? Will I have to stop?

Steven: No, keep going. At first I would find that thoughts would come into my head, and in the early days they did distract me, but now when I have thoughts I just let them pass through my mind and don't pay any attention to them.

I was happy to watch Steven explain what he had learned. Talking to students at the beginning of their development gave him a little confidence. He had already learned this stuff, so he didn't feel he had been put on the spot. It's always so much easier to stand up and speak in public when you actually know what you are talking about.

Our afternoon session was based on the practice of asking your guide to let you be aware of them, using the calling card as identification. Many of the people present had been practising this for a year, as they had been to the previous workshop. Some still hadn't managed to make a connection with their guide, and it was refreshing to hear their honesty. I always appreciate people who say they can't get something. It gives me something to work on.

One man, called Thomas, found it really difficult to get anything from this exercise. He just felt that nothing happened, but said he would carry on practising because he would like to feel what the others had felt. He was a very tall man who at first glance looked serious and stern, but I got the feeling that he was very soft inside and my gut told me that he would do OK, with the right coaching, in the next modules.

The following day we moved on to sitting in a circle. Everyone, even Doubting Thomas, could feel the difference in the strength of energy when we sat them in four circles of ten and let them build up the power. It was amazing that even the students who already had experience in mediumship were more than happy to do this and not try to stand out, as would often happen in workshops or seminars.

For me it was good to watch everyone learning the slow way – the proper way, as far as I was concerned. No one seemed to want to rush, and that was good. They all understood that it would take years of doing these practices to gain a true understanding of spirit. I encouraged them to exchange details and form groups to practise between modules.

The next exercises, 'Sitting in Circle', 'Meeting your Healing Guide' and 'Sensing Emotions', were equally well received, with most of the people picking up something in at least one of them – oh, except for Thomas. I had Steven take notes of everything people said, so I would know where to concentrate my efforts for the second module, and this also gave me a guide as to which students were beginners and which were more advanced.

We knew we had a great group of people who were all willing to work, so we dished out homework for them to do during the three months until we saw them again. I don't think I've ever seen people so keen to work in my life, and this really was good. Not only that, but almost all of them made contact and formed groups to meet together once a week and sit in circle. Those who had to work on their own were told just to practise the first two exercises, 'Sitting in the Silence' and 'The Calling Card', which they seemed happy to do.

Remember, I put these teachings together for a young man who was mixed up in his concepts about mediumship and needed to find direction. I was already seeing a great change in him. Now I wanted to make that same change in as many of the students as I could.

The Second Module

The second module we had planned for our German students was still in keeping with Steven's own development. He had been getting good results in his healing practices with Jim and seemed to be a natural healer. In fact he was one of the strongest healers I had ever worked with. I never told him at the time, though; it would only have polished his ego and we didn't want that.

The next exercise emphasizes setting the ego aside, because what we are aiming at is to allow ourselves to be overshadowed by our healing guide, to let them do the healing through the use of our body, which at that point simply becomes an instrument for spirit to use to get better control of the healing.

Many of the great healers of the past would work in full trance. My old friend Albert Best was an outstanding medium and was known throughout the world for his amazing gift, but what fewer people knew was that he was equally outstanding as a healer. He had a healing guide called Dr Wong who literally took him over and performed tremendous feats of healing. On occasion, Wong actually spoke Cantonese to those who could understand the language. As my old friend Albert could speak no language other than English, this was great proof that Wong was authentic.

It can take years to develop the trust to give that much of yourself to spirit, but in this module we aimed to help the students to start developing that trust.

The students explained that they had been using the earlier techniques in our absence and the results had been very good for most of them. It showed when we took them through the exercise of getting to know their healing guide: almost all of them felt the new sensations and found it quite easy to distinguish between their spirit guide and healing guide.

Only Thomas didn't really get anything much, but he was happy to tell us that he had sat in a circle now with several other students and that he was happy to do all the practices and would keep working on them until he got something. I decided to ask Steven to take him on his own and work with him. I felt that they might create a stronger energy force in a more intimate setting. So Steven and Thomas went to a room above us and began their practice, which was to help Thomas sense his guide's calling card, as there was no point in him trying the new stuff if he couldn't get past this

point. He was willing to go off to work privately while I prepared the rest of the group for the next exercise, which was the actual practice of healing.

In this practice we are looking at two different aspects of spiritual healing. The first is the practice of physical healing, or the laying on of hands. This is when a healer will work directly on the patient's body and might be drawn by instinct to an area which needs healing. Either the healer will feel that they wish to move their hands from the starting position to an area they feel drawn to, or in some cases they might feel a sensation in their own body which tells them they want to heal that area of their patient.

The second aspect of healing which might occur in this exercise is that the student might feel they are guided to lift their hands out into the aura of the patient, either because the area which needs healing is a sensitive part of the body that it would be inappropriate to touch, or because the problem is more to do with the emotions of the patient. I have always found that I am drawn to work out in the aura when the healing is of an emotional nature.

EXERCISE: WORKING WITH YOUR HEALING GUIDE
· ·

Working in pairs, you will each take a turn working as the healer and the patient.

One student will sit in a chair and act as the patient and the other will stand behind them and practise the healing.

Those sitting are asked to do nothing other than relax throughout the exercise.

Those standing are to begin by placing their hands on their patient's shoulders.

Student standing, take a deep breath and relax. Close your eyes.

Let go and clear your mind in preparation to link with the healing spirit around you.

Allow yourself to feel clear and relaxed.

When you feel ready, ask your healing guide to move into your space.

Welcome them and take a moment to feel the adjustment of energy.

When you feel properly connected, ask your healing guide to impress you to give healing energy to the patient in front of you.

Give them permission to guide you in the way they would like to heal through you.

Feel whether there is any energy building around you, either in your hands or elsewhere in your body.

Ask that this energy be channelled through you into the patient.

Be aware of your feelings and register anything you feel in your own body during this practice.

Let your hands be guided and the healing guide take as much control as possible.

Try to work out whether you are picking up on pains or sensations which were not there before you began.

Remember any pictures or thoughts which come into your mind, as they might be important to the patient later.

Always allow your hands to move when impressed to do so.

When you feel that the session is closing, direct your hands back to your patient's shoulders and take a deep breath.

Staying focused but relaxed, become more aware of the room, and with each breath bring yourself back to where you are.

Take a moment to remember anything you feel has happened to you during the healing.

Check that your patient is OK.

When you are both ready, sit opposite each other and share what you felt.

. . . .

I always look for ways of working spontaneously, and just in case any of the German students had preconceived ideas before they began this exercise, I moved them round. This was done by telling them to stand behind the same partner as in the previous exercise, and then, just when they thought they were ready to begin, I moved them all one place to their right, at first much to their amusement, but every time we did the exercise after this some would try to second-guess me, so I never kept it the same. I would move them three to the left or two to the right, and so on.

It is important that you are spontaneous in these exercises and that your mind is clear. If you really have no idea about the person you are working with in the early stages of your development and then get something which is accurate for them, it builds your confidence and your trust in the spirit who is working with you. You know they are giving you information you couldn't have known before you began.

By now, the feeling among our group was energetic and enthusiastic, to say the least. A lot of the students had attended many workshops, but so many reported to me that there had never been much of a system to the teachings they had received, and that they were grateful to be taught in a slow, deliberate way. And they loved the fact that I had encouraged them to form little groups to practise in between the modules.

Even Thomas, though he said he still couldn't feel his guide's calling card, loved the atmosphere of the circle he was sitting in every week and the company of his fellow sitters. He felt that something was pulling him towards the subject and that he had to continue and work out a way to bring down his barriers.

It was his logical, thinking mind that he couldn't get past. He told Steven that whenever he asked his guide for the calling card, his hand kept moving in a sort of spasm and that was putting him off. I think Steven nearly laughed out loud when he heard this because he knew at once that this was the actual calling card and that poor Thomas was missing the point completely. But just to be sure, he took him through the exercise again, and what happened when he asked Thomas to bring his guide through? His hand began to spasm.

Working with the Chakras

Many people who study metaphysics and Eastern practices of meditation talk about the energy centres, or chakras, which can be found in the human aura. They operate like transmitters and receivers of the subtle energy around us and when a person is low in themselves, a healer can sometimes feel that their chakras are out of balance or very closed. When the energy centres are functioning well, they run in a straight line down the body. When out of synch, they may be located to the side of this central line.

Our aim in the next exercise was to locate the chakras and, where possible, give them healing energy. The idea was to bring back balance and rhythm to the energy field.

EXERCISE: BALANCING THE CHAKRAS
· ·

As in the previous exercise, one student will sit and relax throughout and be open to the healing which is about to begin.

The second student will begin the exercise by standing behind their partner and lightly placing their hands on their shoulders.

Student standing, allow your mind to relax to the point when you can feel the peace and stillness within you.

When you feel your mind is clear, ask your healing guide to come into your space. Wait until you feel their presence before you continue.

Ask your guide to direct you into the patient's aura.

Feel your hands gently move off their shoulders and into the space around them.

As you are now in a higher state of mind, you may actually sense the aura through your hands as a solid or tangible substance.

Take a moment to feel this substance and be aware of any warmth or vibration in it.

Take a step to the side of your patient, either to the left or the right, whichever feels more natural to you, keeping your hands away from their body at all times but still holding the connection with their aura.

Place one of your hands in front of the patient's body and one behind it, both out in the aura.

Ask your guide to help you locate the energy centres and allow your hands to be guided up and down the auric field in the centre of the patient's body, from the lowest point beneath the stomach area up to the crown above the head. Always keep a distance from the actual body and never touch it physically.

If you feel your hand being pulled away from the centre line, follow the movement until you get a sense of the vibrating chakra and direct it back into place, using the healing energy which is being channelled through your hands.

Where there is any sense of erratic movement or vibration in the aura, again use the healing energy to bring calm.

Be aware of your own peace of mind in this state and channel this into your partner's aura too.

Create harmony as your hands pull the energy centres into place.

When you feel that you have generated a rhythm which feels more at one with you and the calm you feel in yourself, step back behind your partner.

Ask your healing guide to step back and thank them for being part of the experience.

Now, ever so lightly, let your hands touch your partner's shoulders, grounding the experience and letting your partner know that you have almost finished.

Both of you, breathe deeply and relax, and with each deep breath, come back to a waking state and focus on the room.

Open your eyes and check on your partner.

Sit facing each other and share what you felt or sensed during the exercise.

. . . .

This exercise is useful for learning what it feels like to work with the subtle energies around you. It also allows you to use your instinct whilst working with spirit, a practice which will be used much more as you go on to develop your mediumship. And learning to sense the otherwise invisible auric energy which surrounds us in a way which makes it feel tangible and solid is the first step to making the invisible a reality.

Steven took this exercise and I could feel him trembling with fear before he started, but something we all have to learn on the pathway to mediumship is that you have to go out on a limb sometimes to reach the fruit of the tree. This was the first time he had led an exercise and he did very well, although, like any good student, he immediately felt he could have done ten times better:

> *Of all the things Gordon had taught me, all the exercises of letting go and trusting in spirit, this had to be the scariest for me. I couldn't believe he had asked me to stand up in public and actually teach the exercise. All I can remember is how much my legs were shaking, and that was just from the thought of it. I wondered how I was even going to stand up.*
>
> *During the teaching I remember I couldn't look at any of the students directly because I was sure they would see my body shaking with fear. But when I let go and got into it, when I really trusted that my guide wouldn't let me down, the whole thing changed and I just remembered everything my development circle had given me.*

At the end I actually realized that this was why
I had been developing, and somehow I sensed
that I had moved on because I had been asked
to face my fear and I had done it.

My German students were doing very well too. There were loads of questions about chakras. Many had learned different things about these centres, but I told them they mustn't start to become too involved with ideas that would pull them away from the teachings, simply because having too much information when you are trying to learn will cause you to become overloaded and confused. It was all about feeling and sensing, I told them, and I was more interested in hearing about how they were using the techniques they had been taught so far.

I think they all got the message that I would not be pulled from the teachings, and the results they reported were pretty good. Even Thomas said he had been able to feel what he thought was an energy centre, although it might have been his imagination! That was OK – it takes time for some people's minds to adjust to the concept that there is more to us than just the physical body – but what most people didn't realize was that this was the first time Thomas had actually spoken up in front of the whole class. I could see there was a change taking place in him.

Because module two deals with healing, there was a real sense of relaxation among the students by the end of the first day. Healing is calming and nurturing and I believe everyone was affected by this and a really good space was being created. Much of the students' desire to prove themselves individually was dissolving away and you could see that there was a common purpose now, which was to grow as a group. Real connections were being forged between them. It felt like a development circle.

Practising Group Healing

Most of the students were sitting together in groups now and I felt it was necessary to give them further instructions on what to do with the energy they were building. It is important for any student to dedicate the spiritual energy they build in their circle to a person or situation where there is need. In our own circle we would always close by directing our energy to people we had heard of that week who were in trouble, or who had lost a loved one, or who were ill, etc. Sometimes we would even concentrate on a particular person's need and dedicate the whole night to them.

In the module we put the students into four groups of ten and chose one person from each group to be the leader.

EXERCISE: GROUP HEALING

The group leader will chose a student from the group and sit them in the centre of the circle. That student will tell the group whether they need healing for themselves or they wish the group to focus on someone they know who requires help.

The group will take a moment to concentrate on this.

When the group leader feels they are ready to begin, they will lead the exercise in going into the silence.

Now, all of you, ask your spirit guide or your healing guide to be present and feel the power building around yourself.

Open up your awareness to feel connected to the circle of people around you and sense the energy of the entire group.

Sit for a while in the power and allow your spirit guide or healing guide to become more connected to you.

Turn your focus to the person sitting at the centre of your circle and concentrate on them and their need at this time.

Try and sense if there is any problem or blockage in their life, or focus on where they have asked you to direct healing.

If you are feeling a condition in your own body, or seeing mental pictures of what needs to be done, take that information and remember it.

Ask your guide to channel healing through you to the person in the centre and just allow it to flow freely towards them.

Visualize all of the people in your group doing the same and try to be open and connect to the entire group.

Feel the power as it builds and flows around the group and moves to the centre like a great force.

Visualize any illness or blockage being lifted away from the person and dispersed and cleared.

Relax your mind and take a deep breath.

Thank your guide for working with you and relax your mind back into the silence.

Breathe more deeply, and with each breath, come back to full focus and be aware of the room and the group.

Open your eyes when you are ready and wait for all of the sitters to come back.

The group leader will ask each sitter in turn how they felt during the exercise and if they saw or felt anything that they would like to share with the student in the centre.

The student in the centre will wait until everyone has given their comments before relating how they were affected.

. . . .

During this exercise, each of the four groups experienced a similar increase in the force of the healing. And in this exercise more than any other, where they were asked to link to either their spirit guide or their healing guide, more of them felt a much stronger connection and a real sense of the spirit's personality.

At the end, I asked each group leader to comment on how their circle had felt. It appeared that in all of the groups there had been an amazing connection. Most of the students had experienced the same things. Where there was a physical problem, each student had accurately experienced the patient's suffering. One group had all picked up on a particular colour as they were channelling the healing, as had the patient in the centre. And in the groups that were directing healing to someone other than themselves, all the students had received images in their minds.

Keeping Notes

One of the things I felt would help me to understand the students was to keep notes on what they said at the end of the exercises. We always took time in the early modules to go round them and ask what had happened to them and make them describe whether they had felt it or seen it, etc. Hearing these descriptions told me where the individual students were heading in their development. For example, the students who were very visual were leaning towards clairvoyance, while those who felt deeply and took on some of the conditions of other people were perfect for healing work. I also learned who was anxious to speak to us and who had to have words dragged out of them, when to leave alone and when to encourage, and so on. Steven and I both kept a notebook, and at the end of each module we would compare our findings. It never ceased to amaze us how close our comments were on each student.

By the end of the second module it was quite clear to me who would go on with the lessons and make them a part of their life in the future. But one of the other things that were developing here was the self-awareness of the students.

6

SELF-AWARENESS

*To open is the nature of spirit, just like the
rose in the light and warmth of summer.
Your circle is the garden and the light
is the spirit, your students are the roses.
So, like the rose, open up and show
the world your true beauty.*
MASTER CHI

Spiritual development is not just about the gifts of healing and mediumship and so on. It is about self-awareness and how we shape ourselves and become better rounded as people. It is as much about our own progress in life as about displaying spiritual gifts.

Lots of questions would come at me or Steven now from the students about their fears, and how they could confront them and overcome them.

One of the students who would ask questions about fear was Lana, a young woman in her early twenties. She was the youngest in the group. Often she would become emotional and just break down in tears, not even able to complete the question she had begun. She seemed so sensitive and compassionate and open to everything that I got the feeling that this world was too coarse a place for her and she would have to develop a much thicker skin to exist in it. It seemed that anything would make her cry. I don't think she realized that you have to be tough in development and that being open might leave her very vulnerable, especially when working with people's sadness and pain. I wanted to see her develop some true grit.

Fortunately, we seemed to have created a space which helped people to feel comfortable enough to express themselves and speak openly about their lives and where they felt they had been held back, or caused their own lack of growth. It was clear that the healing energy we were working in was bringing about lots of shifts. There was definitely more developing here than mediumship and healing.

Much of what was happening was a reminder to me of how much my mind had had to open when I was in the first few years of my development class with Mrs Primrose. I had brought all my own fears and restrictions to the class, and not much truly happens until we ourselves recognize what they are. It was the same for Steven. I believed he had a gift and with proper teaching could use it to aid others. But not much would happen for him if he did not overcome his drawbacks.

My work with Steven has helped me to understand how my own teacher felt whilst teaching me. I now know that she must have been very patient because even though she always saw that I would make a medium, she could not unleash me on the public while I was harbouring so many insecurities.

She told me that before I could truly heal others, I had to heal myself. For several months I simply had to ask my healing guide to come and help me heal myself.

I did as my teacher asked, and many things occurred during these sessions, most of which involved remembering emotional episodes from my past and learning to understand them. So often I had experienced emotions that I had just buried somewhere inside myself. I'm sure most people do this, but when you are hoping to serve spirit, and to work with people who might be vulnerable, then you must try to become more emotionally and psychologically robust. Remember, there are no shadows in the spirit world and there is nothing worse than trying to help people who are mixed up emotionally while holding fear, anger, jealousy or hatred inside yourself.

I have said so many times to many people on the spiritual path, 'You must be strong in yourself to help others. People who are in the emotional sea need someone who can pull them out, not someone who gets in with them and gets dragged away by the tidal wave of human emotions. We have to become emotional lifeguards.'

It is important to understand that spiritual work comes with a lot of responsibility. At all times we must be aware of other people's needs, so that we can truly assess whether or not we are the right people to help or heal them. Equally, we must always have our own reality checks and be aware of where we are and if we require helping or healing.

The next exercise shows you how to use your circle as a safe place from which to go back and find some of the emotional baggage you might have left in a deep, forgotten part of your mind. Once again, this is a good exercise to use as a group when you are just at the start of your development, because it is a good idea to accept that you are all developing because you aren't perfect, and the beginning is a good place to look for your faults and try to fix them.

EXERCISE: CLEARING THE CUPBOARDS OF YOUR MIND

Sit in a circle and choose one person to be the group leader.

Join your hands together and go into the silence as a group.

Feel the energy building and moving through your hands, connecting you to the rest of the group.

Often you will feel a very strong vibration around your body. Be aware of this vibration and direct it with your mind in an anti-clockwise direction around the circle.

Sit in the energy and become accustomed to the sense of power and vibration.

Send out thoughts to your spirit guide and healing guide, asking them both to join you in this sacred space.

Welcome them into your energy field and ask them to be watchful and guide your contemplation.

Be at one with yourself and feel the strength of the circle and how safe you are right now.

Allow yourself to go back to a time when you experienced deep emotions, a time when you had difficulties that left their mark on you.

Replay those events in your mind and be aware of the emotion that was at the heart of them. Was it fear or anger, sadness or loneliness, or even hatred or disappointment? Isolate what you felt at that moment.

Now look back at that time and use the power of your circle to lift the emotional memory out of the deep part of your mind and into the centre of the circle.

With the help of your spirit guides, channel healing force towards this old emotional wound and see it healing in front of you.

Allow it to be cut free from you and give it to the power of your circle to be dispersed into the ether.

Feel the freedom that comes when you release this old memory, when you let it go and allow spirit to dissolve it.

And now say to yourself, 'Gone, gone, forever gone.'

Relax your mind, dedicate the energy which remains in the circle to someone else and feel the power of healing rush through you and towards another.

Breathe deeply and relax your mind.

Thank the spirits for being a part of your circle and for their help.

When you feel ready to do so, open your eyes and wait for all the sitters to do the same.

When you are all back and ready, the group leader will ask each person to relate how they felt during the exercise and how they feel now.

. . . .

Many of my students became emotional during this exercise, as you can imagine. Going into the deep recesses of the mind can be painful, but giving ourselves permission to let go of emotional baggage really does lighten the load, and the relief we feel helps us find more peace and contentment.

I found that out when I was in my first private home circle. Sitting in this spiritual environment often brought up emotional baggage in one or another of us. This always occurred whenever the sitter concerned was going through a period of growth in their life. It seems to me that this is a natural spiritual evolution which we have to go through in order to grow and expand. The spiritual closet is no place to keep skeletons.

Quite simply, when we sit in the light of spirit, at some point we will begin to open. And though it may be painful at times, the advantages of becoming open are very rewarding. Remember that when even the smallest amount of sadness or anger leaves our heart, space is created for happiness to come in.

Absent Healing

Many years ago I was taught by my old teacher that I could heal people from a distance, not just when I was sitting across the room from them. In fact the spirit energy we work with in healing can travel across continents. I know that to be true because I have tuned in to people I have known to be sick in Australia and America, to name just two places, and they have felt the benefits of the healing – and sometimes they didn't even know I was doing it.

It is said that Padre Pio, the Catholic priest who was a famous healer, could project himself great distances to heal people while never leaving his room physically. Many people reported seeing him standing over them during an illness and then became well quite soon afterwards. And my friend and teacher Laura, an incredible trance medium, has found herself standing beside patients in hospital giving healing energy to them, again whilst her body has been somewhere else.

Whether or not a healer actually feels the sense of travel or not, their mind can definitely link with patients at vast distances and effect healing on them. I have been practising this form of healing, called 'absent healing', since I was in the early part of my development, either on my own or as part of a circle, and have had amazing feedback from patients.

I taught Steven to do this when he first practised healing with Jim. One of the many reasons for it was to help him develop a more compassionate way of thinking when he did his spiritual work. He was a natural at it and I asked him to share one of the more astounding episodes with the group:

In the early stages of my development with Gordon, just when I first started to practise healing, I had a call from my sister Kelly. She knew what I was doing and asked me if I could send some healing to her husband Danny, who was very ill at the time.

I went off to my bedroom and sat on the bed and began to tune in to my brother-in-law. First, I tried to remember exactly what he looked like. Then I began to visualize that I was standing beside him.

All of a sudden I found myself standing in the hallway of my sister and brother-in-law's home. This really freaked me out, so I opened my eyes.

When I closed my eyes again, I found myself standing in my sister's hallway once more. I didn't open my eyes again this time; instead I walked forward into the front room and there was Danny lying on the sofa, only the sofa was in a different place from where I remembered it being – it was on the other side of the room, against the wall.

My brother-in-law was normally a clean-shaven man, but when I put my hands out towards him to begin the healing, I could actually feel a few days' stubble on his face. I stood there healing him for a while and then I found myself back in my room.

Without thinking, I switched on my mobile phone, which had been off during the healing. Right away my sister rang me and asked if I was wearing a white T-shirt and light blue jogging bottoms. I told her that I was and she sounded shocked. She told me that I had appeared for a second in her hall, wearing the clothes she had described, and then had vanished and reappeared.

I asked her if she had moved her sofa and she said yes, that she had moved it the day before, why?

I told her that I had been doing healing on Danny just before her call and that I had seen inside her home, and then I asked her if he had shaved that day because I had been able to feel his stubble in my hands. Now it was my turn to be shocked – she replied that he hadn't been able to shave for the past four days.

*Danny did get better quite soon after this
episode and I learned that if the intention to
heal is strong enough, part of my mind can
travel to a sick person and I don't even have to
leave the room.*

Quite an amazing experience, I thought. But I already
knew that Steven had abilities and that this would just
be the beginning. His healing was becoming so strong
that many of the students were asking if he would
carry out healing with them in the intervals between
exercises, and all were very impressed by the amount
of power that would pass through his hands.

Remember, though, that he said, 'if the intention to
heal is strong enough' – this is the real key to success
as a healer, and even as a medium. You must truly want
to do this.

With the students, we practised absent healing sitting
in one large circle with our hands linked together. I did
this because every week in our own circle we send
out absent healing as a group. But it can be done as
Steven did it, on your own from your bedroom. You
don't have to be anywhere special. Absent healing is
like prayer in that way: anyone can do it anywhere, as
long as they have faith. The difference is that absent
healing is something you direct from your own mind, or
ask your healing guide to help you direct, whereas with

prayer, in most cases you are asking a higher forcer to do something which you are not a part of.

EXERCISE: ABSENT HEALING
. . . .

At the outset of this exercise you must have in mind a person or a situation which requires spiritual healing. Contemplate this for a moment.

Begin to breathe deeply and go into the silence.

Take your mind down into that part of you which is still and clear.

Feel the power building around you as you become still and your mind begins to empty of thoughts.

Sit in the power for a moment to adjust to the stronger vibration.

Ask your healing guide to come into your sacred space and link with you.

Become aware of the healing guide's sign or calling card and sit still until you feel completely at one with the guide.

Bring to mind the healing you wish to do and begin to

visualize something which is familiar about the person or situation in question.

Concentrate on this for a moment and allow it to become stronger and more real to you.

Try to reach out to the person or situation with your mind and channel the power you are sitting in to them.

Ask your guide to join you and increase the energy which is flowing through you.

See your person or situation being bathed in the healing energy which is pouring from your hands at this time. Give this energy freely and with compassion.

When you feel that you have given what you have to, see your hands coming back towards you and relax.

Ask your guide to step back and thank them for the assistance.

Send out any remaining energy to anyone who needs it at this time and know that the guides in the circle will direct this.

Relax and begin to breathe more deeply, filling your lungs with air. Become more aware with each breath you take.

When you feel more focused, open your eyes.

I know for a fact all the students enjoyed this exercise because everyone wanted to know how often they should do it and could it be done on your own, etc., even though we had told them all those things before we began!

The fact that we were all working together and sending healing as one unit made us feel very bonded. I left the group with a little piece of homework that would mean we would be connected every week: I asked them to join me and my circle in a practice of group absent healing across the continent. Everyone said they would take part. Neither distance nor the time difference could divide us if we all had the same intention to heal.

It was done, our second module was complete and I believed it to be even more successful than the first. A weekend isn't long enough to teach all that there is to learn about spiritual healing, but I knew for a fact that every piece of knowledge imparted over the last two days would be used over the next few months and on our return our students would have made further progress.

Steven also seemed to be very up after his first outing speaking in public. It made me remember the first time I was allowed to get up in public. Even though I was terrified, the letting go, the leap of faith or whatever, seemed to release something and elevate me to a higher level. Now Steven was so happy and relieved I wasn't sure he even needed to be on an aeroplane to feel that he was off the ground.

7

CIRCLE WIDENING

*People ask spirit to guide them, but sit
and wait for the answer to appear.
Sometimes you have to let the spirit move you
to be in the right place to receive the answer.*
MASTER CHI

7

CIRCLE WIDENING

On the way back to Frankfurt airport Steven and I went over all that had happened and discussed the students and who had done exceptionally well and showed real potential. I remember feeling quite happy with my lot, but things were about to get even better.

Just before take-off the air steward came up and asked me if I was Mr Smith. A bit puzzled, I answered, 'Yes.' What was this about? He asked me if I was travelling alone or with company. In response, I simply pointed to Steven, who was looking every bit as bewildered as I was.

The steward then told us that there were seats waiting for us at the front of the plane and asked us to follow him.

When we were seated in business class, we both just smiled and thought, 'There you are – the spirit world looks after its own!'

The steward's name was Paul and it turned out that he was very interested in mediumship. He explained that he had read some of my books and seen me demonstrate mediumship. So he had recognized me and wanted to offer us these seats as a way of thanking me for the good work I did. It was the perfect end to our trip!

During the flight Paul came and chatted with us about mediumship. It seemed he had been interested in it for much of his life. He was very friendly and open, and I had a really strong feeling of connection with him in much the same way that I had felt when I first met Steven.

Near the end of the flight, I told him that I had a tour of theatres coming up where I would be demonstrating mediumship and that if he ever wanted tickets, I would get them for him. He thanked me, but said that he had seen many demonstrations and what he would really love to experience was what it felt like to sit in a development circle. He had never done this, but had read about it in many books about mediumship. 'Just once would be enough,' he told us. Steven took his number and said he would be in touch and we both thanked him very much as we left the plane.

How strange, I thought. Jim and I had recently been wondering if more people would be joining our circle soon. We have an understanding with spirit when it comes to the circle, which is that we will allow spirit to guide the people they wish to develop to us. Although I wouldn't make such a decision based on one meeting with a person, I liked how the encounter with Paul had come at the end of a spiritual seminar, almost as though it was a continuation of it.

It really had been a great weekend and to have it finished off like this was just the icing on the cake. I love my work as a medium and I love to teach people about development and help to make things clear for them, and the modules we were doing for the German students were becoming very rewarding.

It was nice to spend time with them, but I always love coming home and getting back to my everyday life with Jim and Meg, my beautiful spaniel, who I knew would be waiting to welcome me home. That always makes me feel grounded.

Talking to Paul about the theatre tour also reminded me that I would have to prepare myself in the coming days to get back into my own mediumship. I had spent so much time preparing the modules and teaching the group that I hadn't realized I would be demonstrating mediumship around the UK quite so soon. That certainly was grounding – more like hitting the ground running!

Two days later I was travelling to the north of England to do the first demonstration in Warrington, which would be followed by two others in that region. I hadn't given a demonstration for several months and the last time I had worked this way I had felt extremely exhausted. But in the intervening months I had been sitting in my circle and now there seemed to be much more of a purpose in me again.

This was something I wanted to get home to my students when I returned to Germany for the third module, which would feature mediumship in public demonstrations. When I wasn't sitting in a circle I really did feel that my mediumship suffered. Others may have their own way of boosting their signal to the spirit world, but I always feel that my work is much stronger and clearer when I am part of a team which works like a battery charging the energy.

The theatre demonstrations went extremely well, and one thing I know is that when the spirit world is connected to me very strongly, I tend not to get tired; in fact I could go on giving messages all night. However, in a theatre someone always pulls you off the stage when your time is up. Good job, really. But I knew that the reason I was enjoying my work again and couldn't wait to do the next demonstration was that my connection to spirit was flowing in the circle.

Sara

Our circle had a new member now. It wasn't the air steward Paul, but Sara, a woman I had known for years. She was in my teaching group at one of the seminars I run twice a year in Eastbourne for the Spiritualist Association of Great Britain. Sara had been attending these seminars as long as I had been taking them. We had built up a friendship over the years and because she was quite advanced, she always sat in my group, because it featured trance mediumship.

I like to know that I have a connection with the people I have in my circle and that we are all of the same understanding of what the circle is about. So, during one of the sessions at Eastbourne, whilst Sara was sitting in the silence with all the other students in the group and I could sense that her guide was linked with her, I formed a question in my mind and sent it telepathically to her guide, asking if they could move her hands. Within a second, both of Sara's hands lifted from her lap and just floated in mid-air.

Then I asked if the guide could make her stand up and walk to the middle of the room, which again happened as soon as the thought went out. All of this was happening while her eyes were closed. She was being controlled by the spirit guide who worked with her. Her body was turned to face me and her head was bowed.

It was amazing to watch this. I was the only person in the room with their eyes open and I was communicating with her spirit guide by silent thought – something I had learned over the years of sitting in circle.

I asked, again in silence, if Sara could link and work with any other student in the group. She turned and headed in the direction of Steven, who was also in a trance state and whose guide was linked to him.

It was no surprise to me when Steven's hands lifted and stretched forward. His fingertips connected with Sara's for a moment before her spirit guide took her back to her seat and sat her down. She was connected enough to let go and follow the impressions from her guide without question.

I knew at that moment she was our new sitter.

Sara had no idea that I had asked all of this, but when I asked her whether she would join our circle, she accepted immediately. She had been asking her guide to lead her to a new circle because she felt she needed to go deeper and let go more.

It all felt right. She joined us in the next session and it felt as though she had been there forever.

Not so for our air steward, though. Steven had misplaced Paul's details and we had no real way of getting in touch with him. Funny, because I really had a very strong feeling about him and it didn't sit with me that this was the end of it. I was sure that he was to be one of our sitters.

Our circle was getting much more intense now and the energy was almost tangible between us; the feeling of spirit in the room was practically physical and we were getting great results each session. My own public work was also getting stronger and all of this was because of the spiritual cell we were creating once a week. We also did the healing link with the students in Germany at seven o'clock our time, eight o'clock their time, and our healing webs were felt by many.

8

READINGS

Neither space nor time affects the spirit world – or men who know the truth.
MASTER CHI

Working as a medium in public can be very nerve-racking, simply because of the pressure you are under to get it right, to prove to people that the information you are getting is coming from a source that can only be the spirit or consciousness of someone in the spirit world. Also, your whole belief system is based on this type of evidence and you are the one responsible for demonstrating it.

This is why I encouraged Steven to start with private sittings. These are just one-to-one readings and are much more intimate and less stressful than working in a public situation. My old friend Albert Best told me they would boost my mediumship if I practised often. He would even find me people to work on, people who had a need and were willing to take Albert's word for it that I was authentic and he saw potential in me, even though I still had a way to go.

I did the same thing with my student: I had him sit with different people who had lost loved ones, and who were more than happy to allow Steven to practise on them.

On one occasion I had Steven do a reading for me. Much to his surprise, he immediately came up with the name of my grandmother, Joan, and shortly after mentioned 'Cameron', which was her maiden name. He also spoke of the Mull of Kintyre, which was where she was born. He had no idea how accurate his reading was and actually thought I was saying I recognized the details just to please him! During that reading there were a lot of gaps, but it showed me he was learning and was getting the evidence.

I would never have taken him onto a public platform without knowing how well he was doing in the one-to-one readings. If you can come through these readings well, you will have the tools you need to take you on to the public demonstrations.

When I thought he was ready, we held a two-day seminar in Basel in Switzerland, where I am proud to say my student got up on the public platform with me and gave messages from the other side – though not, of course, without some initial reservations:

> *I had given messages before in one-to-one situations and I was fine with that. I would even say that I enjoyed it. But the first time*

Gordon put me on the platform I was nervous and tried to get out of it any way I could.

I always somehow knew that I could do this, but I was afraid that my nerves would get the better of me and that I wouldn't be able to get it right because of that. It took me a while to see that everything I was concerned about was to do with me and nothing to do with the people who had come to try and get a link with a loved one on the other side. As soon as I thought this, I remembered what my development had taught me: that I was the channel in this type of situation, just a microphone for a spirit to contact their grieving relatives.

It all came back to one thing, and that was trust. Gordon told me just before I went on that I really should trust my guides by now and that they would never let me down if I sincerely wanted to serve them. Again this told me how little of me personally would be in the demonstration and that I just had to put my body in front of the audience and let spirit do the rest.

I knew in my heart that I wasn't there to get it right for myself, or to be told that I was a good medium, but to help and heal, to connect with feeling and compassion, to pass relevant information from the spirit to the recipient.

The great reward for trusting in spirit is the amazing buzz you feel when you know that a part of you has been used to help others.

I was so pleased that all the lessons and progressive practices we had done with Steven were proving to work. He had taken the time to sit and digest each lesson and used it to build a link with spirit and confidence in himself.

It's amazing how fast time flies when you have so much going on in your life. I could hardly believe it when Steven told me that our next module in Frankfurt was coming up within a week.

The Third Module

What is the gift of clairvoyance, you ask. Well, it means 'to see clearly'. Often it is not what a person sees which is clouded, but more how they describe it; therefore, clear communication is the skill which must accompany the gift.
Master Chi

All of my young life, before I developed with Mrs Primrose, I had premonitions and sensed people's emotions without knowing why. In development we need to know why such things occur to certain people and not others, and what we can do to use these events positively. So our third module was about psychic impression and mental mediumship.

When sensing episodes and emotional experiences in a person's life, the person tuning in is using their own psychic gift of reading others. This depends on their own sensitivity and intuition. A medium, on the other hand, is looking to open up a link to someone in the spirit world to give them information that is helpful to a person. In the form of mediumship which we call mental mediumship, the information all comes through the mind of the medium, although it is being transferred from the consciousness of the spirit on the other side.

Many times I have been asked what the difference is between a psychic and a medium. This is how I explain it: all mediums are psychic, but not all psychics are mediums.

Spiritual development will make you more empathic, whether you ask for it or not, and there is a very strong psychic element to empathy. It is a small step from being aware of how others feel to seeing an outcome for them based on your feelings.

The first exercise of the third module allowed the students to try to exercise any empathic or psychic gift they had. It was something I had worked on with Steven when I realized that his healing was progressing. Through the wish to heal others, he was developing empathy and I wanted to see if he could pick up information about people without linking with his spirit or healing guide. I wanted to know if he was able to sense the situations around them and maybe even make predictions about them. All of this type of sensing is of a psychic nature and you need to be able to separate it from mediumship.

Once again, the students were arranged into two large circles, an inner and an outer, for this exercise. Their seats were positioned so they were sitting facing each other, and all of the students in the outer circle were asked to practise the exercise on their opposite partner in the inner circle, who was to stay alert and be open to the reading.

EXERCISE: PSYCHIC READINGS
· ·

Readers, take a moment to relax and clear your mind.

When you feel relaxed and clear-minded, take your partner's hands and be aware of the first emotion that comes to you.

Do you sense any turbulent emotions or confusion in your partner's life, or do you sense joy and contentment?

Look for the origin of whatever emotion you sense.

You are looking for time-lines in the person's past where the emotion you have become aware of first began.

Try to visualize events that happened around this time which can be verified by your partner.

Using your own body and mind to receive this information, try to build as clear a picture as your mind will allow.

When you are sure of what you are picking up, communicate as clearly as you can to your partner what you feel, and also if you see anything in your mind.

If you find that the information you're picking up is not accepted, clear your mind and try again. Be sure you are not stuck in your own mind.

When you have information which is accepted, use this to look more deeply at the person's life.

First look for some evidence of their current life which they can confirm. This will show that you have a connection with them and the events of their life. Try to be specific and look for times and dates to build evidence into what you are sensing.

Communicate anything you feel or see to your partner and wait for their reaction.

If your information is understood, then move on to the next step. Where there is uncertainty, ask for a clearer picture in your mind, but communicate everything that is happening to you at that moment.

Allow your partner to answer you when you have given them information, but don't allow them to feed you with things they want to hear. It is your job to sense information about them.

Ask in your own mind what relevance the information you are sensing from the past has to the here and now. Use this link to find out where they are on their path at the moment.

Again using your intuitive mind, ask yourself if you can guide them or assist them. Think like a healer when you ask this and let your healing nature guide you to the appropriate answer.

With each question you ask, try to be spontaneous when you answer. In this exercise, usually the first thought is the best thought.

When you feel that you have passed all the information that is relevant and helpful, thank your partner and stop the exercise.

. . . .

Twenty readings were done in Frankfurt and only two people found that they couldn't get a link and didn't continue with the reading. In both cases these readers were very honest and said that they never actually felt anything. I would have been surprised if all of the group had made connections with their partners, but listening to some of the information we gathered at the end, it was pretty impressive on the whole.

Would you believe it? Thomas *wasn't* one of the students who couldn't establish a link. In fact, his reading was one of the most accurate. It was interesting that he found it hard to get a link with spirit, but in the psychic exercise he was a natural. He told his partner that she had had troubles in recent years with a certain member of her family and that it had caused her great upset and even loneliness. He correctly identified who the person causing the disturbance was and gave the exact time when the upset had occurred. Furthermore, he went on to say that the incident had been cleared up two weeks earlier and that the lady was now in a much better place in her life and that he felt things were back on par. The information was particularly useful as the lady had been wondering if she had done the right thing.

This was good psychic evidence and was used in a compassionate way. The other important thing about this reading was that Thomas had used his healing sense to look for positive information. Many psychic initiates have the ability to pick up on information in a reading correctly, but communicate it badly, leaving the enquirer at a loss or confused, or even disturbed because they don't hear a solution or a positive outcome.

There are many responsibilities that come with psychic gifts, and students should be made aware of them before they ever think of taking them from the class to the public. One man I met many years ago became almost addicted to a psychic reader who constantly told him worrying things about his family. Some of the things were correct, even specific, but she very often left him hanging with more questions and definitely more anxiety than when he started.

Though this was only an exercise for people in development, from the outset I wanted all of the group to know that as we moved into areas where people would come to depend on what we said, we should learn to trust our instincts and be very clear about what we were saying to people. In my life I have come across so many people who have become dependent on psychics and mediums to the point where they can't think or act without their say-so.

This was a good opportunity for the students to recognize the relevance of the course we were plotting. Practising healing before moving on to readings sets a tone for the developing medium. You have to care about what you are doing and those it will affect. Healing and bringing about positive results in people should be the core of all that you aspire to do.

The whole group was delighted to know that Steven had been working with me in Switzerland, and to hear that he had successfully given messages from spirit in public. I believe it showed them that with dedication and practise, they could make similar progress. They also noticed that Steven's confidence had grown since the last module. He was becoming an inspiration!

Mary Armour's Checklist

Talking of giving spirit messages in public, many years ago one of my good friends and colleagues, Mary Armour, a very sought-after medium and tutor, created a workshop which she used all over the world. It was called 'The Medium's Toolbox'. As part of this, she created a checklist for students to use when delivering a spirit message.

The first time I saw her use this I was impressed by how quickly the students were able to work with it. I have used it myself many times since in workshops. I even sent Steven to Mary for lessons in building messages, because she really knows how to make students dig deep to get results. He still uses the checklist today because it helps him to look for intelligent, informative answers which leave the sitter feeling they have had evidence from a relative.

Each of the students in Frankfurt was given a copy of the checklist and asked to study it in readiness for the next exercise:

1. First find out if you are communicating with a male or a female in the spirit world.

2. Ask for a name, either their own name or a surname which is relevant to the sitter.

3. Ask how they passed to the spirit world and when.

4. Ask if they have a birthmark, a scar or distinguishing mark that would be recognized.

5. Ask if there is a significant date, either a birthday the sitter would know or a special anniversary which would be relevant.

6. Ask them why they have come.

7. Ask what is their message for the sitter.

8. Ask if they can make you aware of anything which has happened since their passing – anything recent which will show the sitter that they are still conscious of life on Earth after their passing.

9. Ask for a special memory held between the sitter and the spirit that will have meaning.

10. Have they met anyone in the spirit world who is connected to them that the sitter would be aware of?

EXERCISE: MEDIUMISTIC READINGS

The students will work in pairs as before, with one acting as the medium giving the reading and the other as the recipient.

Students who are the medium, sit still for a moment, relax and go into the silence.

It should not take long to achieve this state at this point, so ask your spirit guide to come into your space. Wait to feel the calling card and make sure that you do feel the presence of spirit before you proceed.

Ask your guide for permission to work with the recipient, and if there is a loved one wishing to communicate.

If you are sure that you have a link for the person, then use the checklist and ask questions of the spirit wishing to communicate.

When you have the first answer, and you are sure that you are clear, let your recipient know what you are getting.

Work your way through the checklist of questions with the spirit you are linked to and try to get as many clear answers as possible.

Always tell your sitter exactly what is happening to you when you get an answer because they may be trying to communicate in different ways. Be aware of all aspects of yourself and any changes which come.

When you are certain that you have tried to allow the spirit to communicate all the information they want to, thank them and ask them to stand back.

Thank your guide also and ask them to stand back.

Take a few moments to focus and relax your mind.

Allow your sitter to share anything they felt was relevant, and to confirm whether they felt you had a link and a message from the spirit world for them.

Remember, the checklist is only a guide to keep the medium on track and focused on trying to get proper evidence for the sitter, and when you are using it you may not get an answer to all the questions you ask. Once you know that you have a strong link to the spirit world and that your guide is controlling what is coming through, you can let go of the list and allow the guide to take you through the reading. I would say this will happen a bit further down the line in your development, though.

The students did very well in this exercise. Again, they loved the fact that we had given them a system to use if they got stuck, one that would remind them of what they were doing and why.

When we questioned the students, we found that some of the readings were very accurate. A woman called Christiana made amazing contact with her partner's uncle, who had only passed six months previously. She immediately identified that she was connected to a man and then got his name and how he died. She found out that he had two daughters and a very strong, positive message was given from him about their lives in the here and now. He also relayed information which only the family knew. Christiana had used the checklist but then went on to describe things that were very personal to her partner and his uncle. All in all, it was a very good reading, and good proof that she was working with the spirit of her partner's uncle.

There were a lot of questions regarding the checklist, but I reminded the students that it was only a tool to keep them on track and guide them when they were learning. The more they became connected to spirit, the less they would need to use it.

One of my favourite things that happened during this exercise came from one of the male students, who admitted that he had only been dragged along to the modules by his wife. He gave some of the most impressive evidence of all and was totally shocked that it was correct. He had never for one moment considered that he could actually do this. The look he got from his wife when we shared his success with the group told me that she was even more shocked than her husband!

At the end of the exercise, I emphasized once again the responsibility we have with this type of mediumship. For those in the group who didn't get a contact, I reiterated that it was important to be open and honest with your sitter about this, rather than try to make things up just for the sake of it. Every decent medium I have met or worked with over the years would tell you that they have had missed readings. This is when no one comes through from the other side, or the medium finds they just can't connect at that time. It can happen for a number of reasons. It may be that the medium just isn't very well tuned in that day. Or in some cases I have found that the spirit world knows that the sitter would not benefit from a reading at that particular point in their life.

I have had days where I have given several private readings back to back and then, for no reason known to me, I just can't get anything for the next sitter. As a medium I am disappointed for the sitter when this happens, but there is nothing to do but tell them this, and not try to flannel them with some sort of spiritual psycho-babble.

Giving Messages in Small Circles

In the time we had between the modules I encouraged Steven to create some new practices for the students in Frankfurt, based on his own development. This way I would also get a sense of where his mind was when it came to explaining mediumship to the group. Though I didn't mention it to him at the time, I wanted him to do some more teaching and give more details of how he was progressing and which exercises helped him most.

At first, true to form, he wasn't sure about creating the exercises:

I couldn't believe it when Gordon asked me to come up with exercises for the next modules. I really thought I wouldn't be able to do it, but I knew that if he thought I could then I would at least have to have a go. I had a connection to my guide, who had shown me so much, and to Gordon, who had given me so many opportunities, so I decided I would just have to put my trust in them and use some of the positive elements I had got from my development.

I thought of how I had always dreaded the public platform and I knew that at some stage of the third module the students would have to demonstrate on their own, so I decided to create an exercise that would be a bridge between doing private readings and standing up on your own. I would have the students stand up and give a message, only it would be within small circles. This, I felt, would make it a bit easier for them.

So it was Steven who came up with this next exercise:

EXERCISE: GIVING EVIDENCE IN CIRCLE

The students are arranged in small circles (in this case, of five people).

One student will simply try to be open and think of someone they have lost.

Remaining students, go into the silence and link with your spirit guides.

When you feel that you are linked to your guide and have felt the calling card, ask them if you may work with the selected sitter.

If the response is positive, using the checklist, ask the spirit if it is a male or female presence who wishes to link, and try to feel the personality of the spirit wishing to communicate.

When you are sure that you have the spirit person there and they are happy to work with you and your guide, ask them one question from the checklist.

Be aware of how you are getting information from the spirit person. Are you seeing it in your mind or are you hearing it? You may be sensing it by way of feelings around your body.

Hold that one piece of information in your mind and then ask if there is any message they wish to pass to the sitter.

Thank the spirit and ask them to step back.

Thank your guides and ask them to step out of your space.

Relax your mind and breathe deeply until you feel that you are completely aware and ready to open your eyes and focus on the group.

Open your eyes and wait for all of the group to join you.

Going round the group from the selected sitter's left-hand side, each student will now explain what they got and how they got it from spirit.

Each student will give the message they got to the selected sitter.

When all students have given their evidence and message, the selected sitter will disclose whether anything that came through was actual evidence from spirit and whether the messages were relevant to them in any way.

. . . .

I was quite surprised by several things that occurred during this exercise. The first was how many of the messages were picked up by at least two of the four 'medium' students in each group. And how five out of the eight groups who got a contact that was verified by the sitter all asked different questions and got relevant answers from the checklist without conferring beforehand. Even in the three remaining circles there was evidence, although it was a bit disconnected.

It was a very good attempt by the students to work clairvoyantly in a circle.

This is the type of thing we did in our private circle in Scotland back in the late 1990s. Our circle then often got one spirit coming through and the seven of us who sat together all picked up a little bit of evidence which, when put together with the others, made a perfect message. I knew that Steven hadn't known that before coming up with this exercise.

The last exercise of the day was carried out in the four circles of ten and each student was given the chance to stand up and attempt to give a message to someone in their group. They were all prepared and armed with Mary's checklist; one by one they stood up and had a go.

Steven and I watched over them and took notes on how each student did. We were beginning to see which students would most probably be good mediums and which would lean more to healing.

It was becoming clearer still that all the students were much more relaxed now and many of them were developing a new confidence in themselves. Lana, the young woman who was so open and often tearful, was one of the strongest at giving a message, and instead of crying and becoming upset when she spoke, she was very sure of herself and appeared to be much more direct and clear in what she said than she had been before. There seemed to be much more strength in her now and there was an obvious positivity in her words which had never been there before.

By now we really were getting to see more of the 40 students' personalities, their weaknesses and their strengths. And even though we would never have expected all of them to want to go on and develop mediumship further at the end of our course, it was uplifting to witness their personal development and improvement in attitude.

The Aura

The second day of the third module was dedicated to working with each student individually and giving them a chance to demonstrate mediumship or psychic reading in front of the rest of the group. But before we did this, we had one more exercise for them to experiment with.

The aura, or energy field, which surrounds the human body can sometimes be detected by the eye. Most people who see this, including myself and Steven, describe it in much the same way: just a faint whitish light beaming around the head and shoulders of a person. At times, some people see flashes of colour in the aura, and certain clairvoyants have devised various systems of detecting whether a person is well or under the weather based on what they see in their aura.

In our course we tried to give as many different examples as possible of the ways in which mediums, psychics and clairvoyants work, and explain, where possible, the workings of and techniques used to improve our spiritual awareness. Not every student would do well at every exercise, but by giving them the chance to try some of the things I had found to be useful over the years, I was adding a variation to their development that might bring out something special in some of them.

I have been seeing auras since I was a child, but it was only when I started working as a medium in my late twenties that it served any purpose. Before mediumship, I just saw people lit up and that was it. In fact I assumed that everyone could see light around people. Now when I work in public as a medium, especially when there is a large audience, it often happens that the aura of the recipient of my next spirit message will stand out more than anyone else's in the crowd.

The other thing about using this exercise is that it adds to the earlier practice of sensing the aura and feeling it in your hands. If you can actually see the aura then it makes what you sensed or felt in the earlier exercise more comprehensible.

EXERCISE: SEEING AND SENSING THE AURA

Using a white or plain-coloured wall as a background, sit one of the students in a chair with their back to the wall, so they are facing the group.

Student in the chair, go into the silence and build your power.

The rest of the group, sit and observe the student, focusing your gaze just around the shoulders and head.

Allow your eyes to relax, almost as if they are going out of focus.

Without trying to look too hard, keep your gaze fixed on a particular point and relax your mind.

With your eyes still open, breathe deeply and take yourself into a more relaxed state of mind.

Student at the front, ask your guide to join you and welcome them into your space.

Feel the presence of the guide as they fill your aura with their own power and light.

Students who are observing, remain in a relaxed state with your eyes open, but relaxed and slightly out of focus.

Be aware of anything you see around the student in front of you, remember what you see, and at the same time be aware if you are affected by what you see. Make mental notes if you feel or see anything different from before.

Student at the front, thank your guide and ask them to step back and move out of your space.

Students observing, try to tune in to the student at the front as they are given their next instructions.

Student at the front, while remaining relaxed, recreate in your mind a situation that caused you discomfort, or a time when you had illness in your life.

Now remember a time when you felt at the highest point of your life and sit in this memory for a while.

Students who are observing, continue to tune in to the student at the front and look for any changes, feelings or sensations.

Everyone relax and breathe deeply to become more focused and aware.

Student at the front, when you are ready, open your eyes.

• •

It was quite amazing how many students saw exactly the same thing during this exercise. Many felt a sense of tightening during the more negative memory, and even managed to tune in to the student when she remembered her illness, the sensations of which were accurately felt by more than half the students. The entire group saw the aura at some point during this exercise and felt that it was much stronger and brighter when the guide was asked to move into it.

Demonstrations

Six months had passed since we had started the very first module and many exercises later we invited the students to give a short demonstration of their psychic and mediumistic abilities before the whole class. I know exactly what that feels like, and Steven, who had so recently done it for real in front of an audience in Switzerland, certainly understood the tension involved in demonstrating in public.

Not all the students wanted to demonstrate at this point, and that was fine by me. I would much rather students put themselves forward than be forced to do it. I have witnessed mediums shame a person into demonstrating before a whole group when they had absolutely no inclination to do it. It can be very embarrassing and puts people off doing it ever again.

No, demonstrating in public is not for everyone. Some mediums feel much more at home when working in one-to-one situations, and it is very important for the medium to be relaxed in what they do. I would imagine that the stress of being forced into giving a message would be likely to block the entire process.

Those students who did get up were the ones we had earmarked as those we thought would be comfortable in a public situation, and because they weren't afraid and knew that it was still a training group, they were very relaxed about the whole thing.

One of the things I stressed before they began is something I tell all training groups when it comes to demonstrating, and that is: remember you have a gift and you are about to share that gift with people. Those who come to see mediums usually do so because they have a need, or because they are suffering due to the loss of a relative and they require your gift to heal them. So, realize that you must open up and be as clear and expressive as you can. Don't close down and go into yourself and close your eyes. People need to see that the medium is confident in their gift, and that confidence will help put them at ease even before you begin.

The medium should never feel they are on trial, or defending their gift. Instead, they should present themselves as anyone would when giving a gift to another person: they should be happy to do it because their gift might change that person's life.

'Be sure of what you do when you demonstrate,' I concluded, 'and talk straight from your heart. Use all the years of practice you have with spirit and allow others to see how much it means for you to help people by sharing this very special gift.'

Pep-talk over, our students put on a great demonstration for us. One by one they got up and confidently introduced themselves and began to display what they had been taught. Some used Mary's checklist to great effect, while others just let go and worked spontaneously and gave what came into their heads. But all the messages that came through were very positive and had enough evidence to convince each recipient that their loved one was communicating.

I got a very accurate message from my father via Bettina, who was one of our more advanced students. She gave me details about him which only I would know and provided many references to things which were happening around my mother at the time. At the end of her message I knew that my father was linked and wanted to give the same type of guidance and advice he would have done when he was with us physically.

A lady called Gisela gave a message to one of the other students which included very strong evidence, including the name of the lady's former fiancé, who had been killed in a tragic car accident several years earlier, the date, year and manner of his death, and even a description of the tattoo he had had on his forearm. The woman she was working with was in tears of joy because she had never had a message from him before, even though she had been to professional mediums in the past. The message was that he was happy she had now found someone else. She had had some concerns about that, so was particularly pleased to be able to lay these to rest.

There were too many good messages to mention all of them, but they inspired the rest of the group because many of them asked if there would be another opportunity to demonstrate in the later modules. They realized that there was a great joy in sharing their gift with others. The entire demonstration was very inspirational and once again we finished the weekend on a very high note.

Steven and I were very pleased with what had happened. Now we were seeing the results of the past six months and all the effort the students had put into their development. It was also good to hear that even more of them were sitting in little circles and more friendships were being created.

I thought back to the first module, when I had wondered whether the group would ever gel. Now the buzz in our seminar room was quite something. Between exercises the noise level was full blast, but it was all friendly noise and it seemed to add to what was happening in the modules. Even our translator, Monica, commented on how the ambience in the room had altered. Sitting in development is great, but when you feel that high energy build in the actual room you are sitting in, then you know you are doing something right.

The students wanted to do as much as they could and I genuinely believe that they would have practised these exercises every day if we had asked them to. It was this kind of eagerness that had filled the room with positive vibrant energy.

9

TRANCE

*Trust me, my friend, when I ask you to let go,
for I will never let you fall.*
MASTER CHI

The idea that our German students were forming circles and really enjoying their development was very pleasing to me. I always believe that the circle we sit in is the strength and fuel for the gifts we develop on the spiritual path.

When Sara joined our circle, the four of us started sitting on a Thursday at seven o'clock and in no time spiritual connections and power were being felt in the group. Whenever we sat in the silence, the atmosphere in the room was almost tangible. Jim and I felt that we had brought something straight from our previous circle in Scotland and reopened it in our new group.

During the later stages of our old circle there was no doubt it was geared towards trance mediumship and a greater awareness of spirit. The sitters often described it as being halfway to the spirit world. There were very few occasions when a message would come for any of the group. It really was more about expanding our minds and letting spirit have more control of our space and use our minds and bodies to let us feel more of spirit and less of ourselves.

To give an example of this, I would just send out the thought that I wanted the spirit guide who was controlling Christine to stand her on her feet. Within a second, Christine's body would stand up. I would then think that she should walk in my direction, and again she would, without pause. No words were ever spoken and this showed the level of telepathy that was at work between Christine's guide and me. The rest of the sitters in the circle were capable of the same level of trance and their guides would all respond in the same way when asked.

I often use this type of telepathy with the spirit guide of a person who says that they can go into trance. It allows me to know how far the spirit is actually in control. When the spirit has use of the medium, they have no problem responding to my silent questions. This is exactly what I did with Sara's guide before she sat with us. The way she responded told me she was ready to come into our circle.

The new circle would go even further than the last, I felt, as even at the beginning we were building a powerful energy and, like the last circle, we were all friends. That is important. When we sit in a spiritual group, we have to trust one another in order to open up completely and allow spirit the use of the space we create. If there is any distrust among the sitters, the spiritual work will be limited. The same would apply if any of the sitters had a fear of letting go and allowing spirit to occupy more of their mind.

When a medium can give themselves to spirit in this way, it shows trust, and I know that when we display such trust we get such a sense of the spirits coming to us that we feel them to be as real as the people around us. It really changes your sense of reality. It is one thing to receive a message from a medium in public, or in a one-to-one session, but when you actually feel the presence of a spirit and in a moment sense exactly who they are and what their personality is like, well, that is taking you away from *belief* and into a place of *knowledge*.

It was becoming more important for me to tell any student that came to a workshop or seminar that they needed to join a circle if they could. Many mediums today offer courses which only involve the kind of mental mediumship exercises we did in module three. There are many circles in the UK which are dedicated to this type of mediumship, yet I know that if they can expand these circles to become much deeper trance circles, then all the sitters in these groups will benefit and grow spiritually.

I don't just want mediums to get messages through a thought process, but to actually feel the presence of the spirit who wishes to communicate. Nor do I want my sitters to just *believe* that there is a spirit world – I want them to *know* that it truly exists, as I do.

Whenever I work as a medium, even in public, I open myself the way I would in a circle. I have learned how to let go and let spirit work through me. What comes out of my mouth is not formed in my head, but passed through me by my guides and the loved ones who want to communicate from the other side. Even if I just have to give a talk in public I never make notes or even think about it, I simply open up to be inspired and allow my guides to use my faculties. That way it becomes more of spirit and less of me; it is much more pure and authentic.

I was taught this by several great teachers in my life – Mrs Primrose, Albert Best and Laura, the unbelievable trance medium, to name but a few. And as I write, all of what they taught me and all of what I have built in my own circles is becoming focused on the here and now. The teachings that are coming through are more about bringing people closer to spirit, and that is why we are trying to take these lessons to as many people as we can.

Before we headed to Frankfurt to start module four, we were invited back to Basel to start teaching the modules to a group there. They had heard from some of the students in Germany how much they were enjoying them and how much they were learning from them. And at the end of the first module in Basel, we were asked if we would go to Geneva and do the same there. This told me that everything was as it should be, and that somehow our own circle was right on track.

The Fourth Module

Our fourth module was based on trance mediumship and the deeper levels of the spiritual circle. It was simply taking all that we had already taught into a deeper state of awareness. The students' link with their guides would now be made in a way that would help them to let go more, and the healing would now involve their healing guides taking more control. We would also allow all the students to show how much they had learned to trust by giving them the chance to give a spontaneous talk to their groups, letting themselves be inspired by their spirit guides.

I let Steven give a talk on letting go because it was something he was able to do more in the circle now, and I knew that he was ready to convey this to the students, as his own view of development had changed and his trust in his guides was becoming stronger. Also, he had just left behind the doubts that many of them would be holding:

When I finally learned to let go enough to allow spirit to use more of my mind and body, it was a truly amazing experience. It was almost too out of this world to describe in words! It was like going into an empty space where I felt completely safe, as if nothing could harm me and I didn't have problems, a kind of nothingness you could say, where you never expected anything and there was no need to achieve anything either.

During this experience I was so out of it, yet I was so aware at the same time. I noticed that there was a dog sitting at my feet. It was a real dog; in fact it was Gordon's dog Charlie. I had never met him but I knew he was in the spirit world. I felt connected to everything but not that concerned, even that a spirit dog was beside me.

Then I felt as though I was sitting in someone else's body and only a part of my mind was in the room somehow. Not only could I feel the other body, but I could feel a personality which wasn't me. I sensed that this personality belonged to a woman, and at the same moment I heard her voice as my head was bending down towards the dog. My mouth almost opened as I heard words being said, saying hello to Charlie. This action snapped me back out of it and my eyes opened and I was back in my body and back in the room.

The experience was so real that it took me a moment to know what was reality, where I had been and where I was now.

Since that first time I have learned to go with it more and the spirit guides feel so real that I can feel what they are wearing. It feels as though I'm wearing them at times. At times this has become so real that it would be silly of me to say it was just a belief. In fact I think it would be like Neil Armstrong trying to imagine what it would be like to walk on the moon one day and then actually doing it for real. It's one of those things where you really have to experience it to understand it.

This gave the students the idea that we were taking them to another level. They had met Steven as a nervous and quite shy student of mine, and now his progress was obvious to them. I could feel that they all wanted to do as he had done and go beyond their limits and trust more in their spirit guides.

Going Deeper

Our first exercise was to be done in circle, so four groups of ten were set as Steven prepared to lead them. I had worked with him almost a year before on how to go deeper into a trance state and he genuinely felt it had helped him, so he wanted to share it with the students himself.

Going into a trance state is not so different from sitting in the silence, but it lasts longer and we focus less on the physical world and connect with our true higher self. When we become our instinctive self, and have no doubts but just are, spirit has a clearer connection to us and we share a reality.

EXERCISE: A DEEPER STATE OF SELF

Sit for a moment in your circle and join hands to allow the energy to flow through each sitter.

Be aware that you are part of a circle, a spiritual unit which is about to open a sacred space for spirit to come into.

Begin to feel the vibration of the energy as it works to find a harmonious tone between all the sitters.

Use your breathing exercises to relax your body and mind until you are aware only of the conscious part of your mind, which is connected to my instructions. Use this part of yourself to tell your physical body to be at peace.

Your body is peaceful, as you have commanded it to be. Tell your mind to be still and clear of thinking. Let any thoughts that come into your mind pass through. There is no need to be attached to them. They are travelling towards the physical world; you are heading in the opposite direction.

Your thinking mind sits at the top of your head, around your brain. Now you will enter into your inner world, at the centre of your being around your heart.

Let your consciousness come down through your being, like walking down a staircase.

Come down one step at a time, slowly and deliberately. Be mindful of every step you take as you descend deeper into your being.

The physical body is at peace now; concentrate on the subtle force which commands and guides it. Let this part of you come down to the heart area, which is now vibrating and pulsing slowly and steadily.

This is the next vibration of the self, which is lighter and more fluid. Be aware of the liquid which gives the body life and take a moment to feel the movement of the heart as it beats and slowly moves the fluid part of your being in a steady rhythm.

Come down to the very centre of yourself – just beneath the heart – where the next rhythm of the self is the air, an even finer substance than the fluid, which is being moved in and out of you at a very slow, steady, harmonious pace.

Feel yourself in tune with the gases which are part of you.

As you become in harmony with this aspect of the self, be at one with yourself here.

The fine light of energy which surrounds the body comes from this part of you. Be aware of how light you feel here and now.

This is your light body, which can connect to the spirit world.

Send out the intention to link with your spirit guide at this spiritual level and welcome them into this most sacred part of your consciousness.

Ask for nothing, just be still and allow the spirit guide
to bond with you. You have created a situation which
allows them to be a part of you and you of them.

Give yourself permission to be as much in this moment
as your consciousness will allow.

Eventually, you will get a sensation that your guide is
moving away from you, leaving you in this quiet place.
Allow this to happen. Think of nothing but stillness.

Now start to come back up the inner staircase, slowly
and deliberately, one step at a time.

Be aware of your breathing, of your heart beating slowly
and of your body resting in the chair.

Breathe more deeply and focus your awareness on your
physical body. Begin to allow it to reconnect to your
mind as you start to come back to the room
more clearly.

With each breath now moving deep into your lungs, you
are ready to open your eyes.

Open your eyes and wait for the rest of the group to
come back also.

Each member of the group will explain what they experienced and a group leader will take notes.

. . . .

This exercise lasted for an hour and all of the students managed to stay with it. In fact, none of them could believe that they had sat for an hour! Both Steven and I are quite used to time disappearing when we sit in our home circle. It feels surreal – you have just closed your eyes and now you are opening them again, and in your head you feel that minutes or even seconds have passed when in actual fact one hour has elapsed.

The fact that the students had encountered this was a very encouraging sign for us, because being in an altered state of consciousness is one of the strangest sensations you can have. This exercise had taken the students to the early beginnings of a trance state, and all of them had experienced it simultaneously. From where I was sitting, I was very aware that this was happening. Even though I remained conscious throughout, I was still exposed to the timelessness which the students felt.

The general message which came back from all the circles was that everyone felt the density of the group they were in. Some felt it was uncomfortable, but managed to stay with Steven and let go further as he took them down to the deeper states of mind. Others said that the reality they experienced when the guide came to link with them was much more physical than they had ever felt it before.

Many people were quite shocked by the fact that they could feel actual clothes and characteristics of their guide that they had never known before, while others saw images or felt that they were in a place where the guide had lived when in the physical world, almost as if they were seeing the memories of the spirit person who was with them.

The exercise left them all buzzing and wanting to do more. I explained that it would still take them years of practice to truly understand their link with spirit, but that they had done so well already because of how committed they were and also because of all the practise they were putting into their own circles between modules. I think they got it by now that one successful exercise does not a medium make, but it was still very encouraging.

A Deeper Link

Your first deeper link with spirit makes everything you did before seem lame. I remember all the times in my first circle when I thought I had had an amazing experience and then something else would happen and I would be astounded.

The first time I made a deeper link with Chi, Mrs Primrose sensed that my guide wanted to make a deeper connection with me and she quietly walked towards me and stood in front of me, guiding everything without words. With my mind elsewhere, I had no sense of the room, but I suddenly felt my body rise up to a standing position. Only I wasn't in it. The actual feeling at that moment was indescribable. I was somewhere in it all, but I wasn't sure where. By that I mean that I was conscious that my body was moving and my hands were moving, but I wasn't doing it. I could see places which were strange to me. It was like being taken back in time and to another country. I could see a woman standing in front of me, but it wasn't Mrs Primrose. It was a nun who was wearing an old-fashioned heavy habit or robe of some kind; I could even smell smoke on it. Later Mrs Primrose told me that this was one of her guides. When I told her how real everything had become, she just smiled.

It was hard to understand at the time, but the longer I sat in development, the more I became accustomed to such happenings, and I began to get used to feeling that I was out of my body and someone else was working mine. It's quite a sensation, to say the least, and that is why it takes a lot of time and trust to be ready for such a thing. This is why I use this slow, progressive training, because I know that we need time to adjust to a different reality and we are not programmed to accept such a thing in one go.

The reason the spirit world requires more of our body and mind is to use our body to deliver information straight from them to people. Spirits can pass information through a medium in a heightened state of consciousness, as they do when they give messages in a public demonstration, but even then the mind of the medium can interfere and introduce doubt into the proceedings. In a trance state, the medium becomes a much clearer channel because there is less of the part of the mind that doubts to interfere.

Before we get to the point where we can be used to channel information directly from the spirit world, the spirit world has to adjust our body and mind. This was what would happen in our first private circle with the telepathy I spoke of. There were many occasions when one of the sitters would feel that spirit was moving their hands, but didn't know why. They just trusted that they had to go with it at the time. But I would be asking their guides to do it by directing a thought to them.

This is what Mrs Primrose did too, although she never told me. One day it just suddenly dawned on me that I was in the position that she used to be in. She used this type of practice with the open circle, and this is how she came to know which students were truly connected to their guide. It also told her who was ready to move on to allow the spirit to come through more and actually channel if it were appropriate.

In the module I allowed myself to go into a trance state and then had Steven telepathically instruct my guide to move my body. He would ask that I be moved to an area in the room which he would point to and then I would be walked there. He never spoke, and as my eyes were closed, I couldn't see him pointing, so I had no idea what he was instructing.

Then he asked some of the students to whisper an instruction to him and he would relay that, via thought, to my guide, who would graciously respond.

The students couldn't believe their eyes at times. For example, when the command was to make me walk backwards, or to walk me in and out of tight spaces without touching a single object, which was interesting considering that the floor was full of people's bags and bottles of water and such. What the students realized was that the spirit world can use a medium in trance to see into our world.

Our next exercise was based on what I had just demonstrated with Steven and my guide. We arranged the group in two circles, an inner and an outer, with each student facing another. The students in the outer circle were to attempt to connect with their guide and the students in the inner circle were to try to make a link with that guide using telepathy.

EXERCISE: TELEPATHIC
COMMUNICATION AND TRANCE

Students in the outer circle, prepare your mind to go into the silence as before.

Take yourself into a relaxed state. Relax the body and still the mind.

Take time to prepare yourself to go down into your inner self, to your very heart, where you exist at a lighter, finer level.

Students facing them, keep your eyes open but relax your mind and try to tune in to your partner and follow where they are in the process.

Feel what they are feeling.

Become connected to them.

Students in the outer circle, when you are ready, ask your guide to join you in the silence.

Sit with them in the silence.

Students facing them, if you feel a connection to your partner, you will now feel a connection to their guide if they have made a link with their medium.

Using your thoughts only, and directing your thoughts to the guide and not the person sitting before you, ask the guide to make a small movement using the medium's body – nodding the head of the medium or moving a finger, etc.

If this occurs then you can ask them to make another small gesture and begin to build up communication using this system.

When you are sure that they are responding to your telepathy, ask a question of the guide which can only have a 'yes' or 'no' answer and ask them to make a response if the answer to your question is 'yes' and not to respond if the answer is 'no'.

Once you have had an answer, mentally thank the guide.

When you feel the time is right, use the same telepathic process to ask the guide to step back and allow the medium to come back.

When your partner is completely back you can exchange information about what happened during the session.

. . . .

After the information had been exchanged between the students, we changed them around and allowed the other students to experience the same exercise.

It was quite a successful exercise, with some of the students feeling that they got good reactions from their partner's guide. There were also those who felt that their partner's guide was there, but they themselves were holding back any movement for fear of getting it wrong. This was good in that they knew they were getting an impression from spirit and realized they were prohibiting the movement out of fear.

Lots of questions followed. The students realized that they still had a way to go before they could allow themselves to step back and let their guide have more of their mind. I reminded them once again that it takes time for a student to trust an invisible instructor. The good thing about these students was that they never really got despondent because they knew they would have a chance to practise the exercises again, and they always accepted that they were still at the beginning as far as development was concerned.

When we are ignorant of impressions from spirit, we are not even ready to open up to development, but when we get the lesson and are afraid to act on it, we are ready to begin. For the first couple of years in my own development I must admit that I had many impressions from my guide which I never followed. Even as a medium I would pick up information out of nowhere and know in my heart that it was right, but I wouldn't communicate it to the recipient. Whenever this happened, though, the recipient of the message would speak to me afterwards and somehow they would mention what they were waiting for. This is how I knew this was a type of lesson from my guide.

Our guides are very patient and we too have to learn to become patient on our spiritual journey. It's not just about learning a lesson or understanding the philosophy, it's about the experience and having the courage to follow what's in your heart and let go of your inhibitions. It's difficult to carve a hard block of wood.

Trance Healing

The next lesson was about trance healing. Again, I must stress that giving a lesson in a subject does not mean for a second that we expect to develop everyone in the group in it. But there were several students in Frankfurt who I could see had the potential to take this further, and it wouldn't do the others any harm to try to let their healing guide come through and work their channel in a session of healing.

There have been many healers whose healing guides have become better known than they have because the personality of the guide comes through so completely when they are healing a patient. My old friend Albert Best was not one of these, as he was very well known as a medium, but the Chinese doctor who would come through him when he was healing, Dr Wong, definitely had his own personality. In the time he worked with Albert they recorded 23,000 successful healings on patients at a clinic in Scotland – and who knows how many elsewhere?

Like any other form of trance work, trance healing can only truly happen when the medium or healer can let go of their mind enough to allow the guide to take control and give the guide enough energy to work with.

We chose the students we felt were closest to doing this to demonstrate the healing. A young woman called Petra was able to let go quite a bit and both Steven and I felt that with a little help from us she would be able to take it a step further. I was going to ask my guide to overshadow me during this and literally control the experiment by leading Petra's healing guide and also creating an energy around her which would give her a stronger connection to her healing guide than she had had before.

In my own early development, Laura, my friend and teacher whose trance work was very advanced, would sit me at her side in the circle and her guide would help my guide. I had been doing this with Steven, too, for the past four years, and it is why he was able to have the kind of experience he described when he first met spirit at a deeper level.

Petra was asked to take herself into the trance state and do nothing but form a link with her healing guide. At all costs she must not try to think about what was being asked of her. The importance of this experiment depended on how much she could let her guide control her mind and body.

Steven chose a student from the group simply by pointing to where he felt Petra's guide should work, and I asked my guide if he would come and link to the work and guide things.

Steven had chosen a woman who was sitting opposite and slightly to the left of where Petra was sitting. I could feel that my guide was already connected to Petra's, and within a second Petra was on her feet and following my guide's telepathic instructions, walking in the direction of the chosen patient.

Her body was guided to the side of the chosen student, and with one thought from Chi, she moved her right hand onto the woman's back, while her left hand worked around her neck and shoulders. The rest of the group were quite astounded by this silent instruction coming from invisible spirit guides.

Standing on the opposite side of the room, Steven bowed his head in Petra's direction to indicate that the healing was over and her body slightly turned to him and her head bowed back to him as she stepped away from the patient. Again, people looked amazed.

I lifted my hand and could feel there was an invisible connection between Petra and me, and between both our guides. So, to further demonstrate to the students that she really was under the control of spirit, I directed her with a hand motion to walk in the opposite direction, back to her seat.

Anyone with their eyes closed would find it difficult to make their way around a very large room with 40 students sitting in a circle, but Petra walked gracefully back to her chair, turned to stand in front of it and then gently sat down.

When we brought her back she was almost speechless for a few moments, trying to find words to describe how she felt. She said there were times when her mind would come in and think, but there was a stronger force there that would 'pull' her body and she would concentrate on this and her doubts and thoughts would fade. She had known that she was walking, but had been aware that there were other spirits connected to her and had actually been more aware of Steven and the spirit guides than the people in the room.

She also described to the group how safe she had felt. She said it had been like being wrapped in a blanket that was safe and warm. She had never felt a trance so strong and she couldn't wait to try it again.

The patient told us that she had felt tremendous heat from Petra's hands during the healing, that she had been suffering from back pain and headaches for years, and had an amazing sense of relief now.

Now it was time to see whether any of the other students could let go in the same way Petra had. We arranged the group into the two circles, creating a gap this time so that if the healer went into a trance they would have to ask the healing guide to come and walk them to the patient. It was not like the walk Petra's guide had had to do, but it would require a bit of trust.

The students in the inner circle sat with their backs to their partners, who would attempt to be guided in trance by their healing guides. Steven would take them into the silence and guide them through the link, while I would watch over and give help to those I felt had a link. Although I never told them I would do this, I hoped that some of them might pick it up. I also do it in my own circle, as it lets me see who is aware and who is not.

Here Steven was speaking only to the students who would do the trance practice:

EXERCISE: TRANCE HEALING

Sit quietly and relax your mind and body.

Be aware of your breathing and nothing else at this time.

Start to go into the silence of your mind and feel how your body relaxes as you do this.

Clear your mind and feel the power building in your sacred space.

Start to come down into the centre of your being and feel the peace as you move towards this higher state of mind.

In this higher state of being you are at one with yourself and clear in your mind.

Take a moment to sit in this clarity and just be.

Ask that your healing guide be allowed to join you and welcome them into your sacred space.

Feel the link between you grow stronger until the guide is a part of your very being.

Ask if your healing guide will take more control of your body and mind for the purpose of healing the patient who is sitting in front of you.

Follow any impressions that your guide gives to you. Let go of your thinking, and any doubts which come into your mind.

Trust completely that you are in safe hands and that it is fine to allow yourself to be guided.

When you find you are connected to your patient, either in the aura or connected to the physical body, allow your hands to be guided by your healing guide and let them do the work.

Be aware of any feelings, impressions or pictures which come into your space during the healing and remember them.

Allow your guide to direct you and make you aware when the practice is over.

Ask them to guide you safely back to your chair and sit you back where you started.

Thank your guide and ask them to step back and allow you to become more aware of the room again.

Breathe deeply, and with each breath become more focused on the room.

When you are ready, you can open your eyes and share your experiences with your patient.

. . . .

This exercise was interesting for several reasons. I was in a position to watch yet still be tuned in to the students. More than half really went with it and created a good strong link which they trusted from start to finish. And several whom I directed energy to responded with a nod of gratitude in my direction whilst still in trance. This was interesting because during the exercise I was walking slowly and silently around the group, so they never knew where I was. Only at the start and finish was I in the same position.

It was quite funny to see some of the students opening an eye for a second to see if they were standing in the correct position. It was clear that they hadn't followed the instructions and made the link in a deeper trance level, but they carried on healing regardless!

Some of the reactions from the patients were encouraging. Some of the healers were accurate in the point of the body they were directed to work on, and some of them even picked up on their patient's past illnesses and operations. It was a good exercise and a good percentage of the students did very well.

Thomas was one of those most connected to their healing guides and he even gave an amazing description of his patient's medical history at the end of the healing when we asked them to share their information. Not so much Doubting Thomas now, methinks!

On the following day we gave talks on mediumship and healing, going over much of what we had covered so far, and had many questions from the students.

One woman asked how she could do more to advance. She genuinely wanted, as most good students do, to put her development to use. I couldn't help but think of Mrs Primrose's answer to me when I had asked the very same question: 'Son, you can never go slowly enough. When you have had more experiences, you will learn from each one what you need to take you further in your development, but you can't create them if they're not there.'

She always had these simple answers to my questions and mostly that was fine, but I must admit to always being infuriated with her when her answer was, 'All will become clear in time, son.' I make sure I never say that to students when they put questions to me now. I think it is because I asked so many questions of my teachers that I heard this answer so much!

The students also wanted to know how they could communicate with their guide the way Steven and I seemed to.

'Well,' I said, 'I have been doing this kind of development and linking with spirit for over 20 years, and practising the work too. But Steven has only been in development for four and a half years and he is getting there, so let him be your aim at the moment and look to achieve what he has in that time.'

Physical Phenomena

The questions, they just kept coming! Some people wanted to know about the more physical types of phenomena – things like materialization mediumship, where the entranced medium works in a very dark room and the spirits use a substance from their body called ectoplasm to mould their image and appear physical in the séance.

I gave some examples of this type of mediumship that I had heard from Albert, Mrs Primrose and other older mediums I knew who had had actual experience of it, but said that we really couldn't expect to produce this kind of phenomena in the modules, as these mediums had sat regularly for years in the same circle to build the type of energy required to produce this.

We did, however, teach the students how to set up a transfiguration séance. This is also done in the dark, but with one dull red light at the top of an enclosed cabinet which the medium sits in whilst going into trance. The purpose of such a séance is for a spirit to use just the minimum amount of ectoplasm, with which they form a skin or mask over the medium's face and reproduce their own facial features.

The students all mucked in to black out all the windows in the room and construct a makeshift cabinet out of black material. We then clipped a small red light to the top front which would shine directly onto the medium's face. A tall stool was fitted into the cabinet for the medium to sit on and all the chairs were placed in front of the cabinet so that the students would have a clear view of the medium.

The idea of this was to let the students who wanted to have a go at sitting in this type of energy do so while Steven or I controlled the proceedings. This was just an experimental séance and we never really expected much to occur; it was more for the experience than anything else. Also, it was important that if people wished to try this sort of thing, they knew how to do it properly and why they would want to.

I sat first, for about 20 minutes, before Steven brought me back. Some students said they had seen my guide and others that they had seen different colours around me, like energy forming. I knew that my guide had come and some of those who claimed to have seen him did give accurate descriptions of what he looked like. But more than generating phenomena, I wanted to go in first to build the energy for others to follow and get a sense of what it felt like.

Six students then had a go at sitting in the cabinet and all of them definitely experienced a different feeling from when they sat in their regular circle. The students watching found that when their eyes went slightly out of focus, they saw more, and many reported the same things at the same time. For these to be classed as genuine physical phenomena, everyone would have to see physical changes to the medium's face, but, a bit like the exercise in seeing the aura, I think that with regular sitting for this type of mediumship some of the students would definitely progress.

However, our main teaching in this module was about how an individual could work in trance and take this into their circle. So, onward to our last exercise of this module, which involved … trance and circles.

Guides Working with Guides

Part of the trance healing experiment we did with Petra was to show how a medium's guide could link to another person's guide and work with them. As I have already explained, this happens in my circle when I link to the other sitters: Chi will come and guide their guides as to how best to work with their mediums.

In this exercise we put the students back into the four circles of ten and chose the most experienced medium in each group to be the leader. This leader was to remain in a waking state, but link to their guide as I had done in the earlier experiment and try to give them control of their group by connecting to the sitters' guides and asking them to give them a particular confirmation.

In this exercise, though, the leader would also intend to help someone they knew who needed healing or, if they felt it necessary, one of the students in the group. They would not say this out loud but try to convey it telepathically to the guides of the students and see if any of them were able to pick up on it. This was actually a good exercise for the people we chose as leaders because all of them ran circles and would benefit from this type of practice.

EXERCISE: WORKING WITH THE GUIDES IN CIRCLE
· ·

Group leaders, quietly take the sitters into the silence.

Using the same technique in earlier exercises, ask them to build the power in the circle.

When you feel that their circle is in a good state of stillness, and the power is sufficient, instruct the group to welcome their guides into the circle.

When the sitters are connected, mentally address their guide with a nod or bow, accepting them into the circle, and wait for them to respond.

Remember, you and your guide are in control of this circle and the other guides coming through will respect this, so never be afraid to acknowledge the guides, but ask them to follow your requests.

When you feel that the spirit guides are all linked to their mediums, and you have welcomed them all into your circle, send out a thought to them and ask if they can assist you in helping the person you have chosen, either in your circle or elsewhere.

Allow the sitters time to sit with their guides a while to feel any impressions which might come to them.

Thank the guides for coming into your circle and, again without words, start to bring everyone back.

Be aware of which sitters react to your thoughts immediately and which don't. If all the sitters come back at the same time, you have had a very good connection in your circle.

If there are people who have not reacted to your telepathy, guide them back using words until all your sitters are back.

Now ask your own guide to step back from the circle and thank them.

Go round your circle individually and ask each sitter to share their experience with you.

. . . .

From the feeling in the room whilst this exercise was going on, we could tell there was a very strong spiritual presence building. Neither Steven nor I were in any way surprised that all of the circles were in such harmony with their leaders. Afterwards there were similar reports from all of them that it was the deepest link they felt they had ever made.

It was really satisfying to witness the students, who had all looked so doubtful on the first day of module one, letting go so much and reacting to the telepathic instructions of the spirit guides. There weren't even any questions at the end – people just wanted to say what they felt. There was an unspoken understanding and no one wanted to break that feeling or disturb the moment. It was the right way to leave the module on trance.

I thought we had taken the students quite a distance in ten months. And I was now talking to Steven as one of the tutors and not so much my student any more. These modules had helped him to grow and express himself, and to gain confidence and respect from the group. This was as much his teaching now as it was mine.

It was strange how, as we walked through the airport on our way home, we both at the same moment began to talk about Paul and wonder if he would be on our flight again, but it wasn't to be. I still thought he would have made a great sitter in our circle, but I knew that spirit would send us the person who was right for us if we only trusted them.

10

WORK IN THE CIRCLE

In the class which has harmony, trust and love,
you may not see teachers, only mirrors.
MASTER CHI

We already had two new people coming into our circle: Craig, who was Steven's age, and Colin, who was to be the elder of the group, we decided. Both were looking for a development circle to sit in and both turned up out of the blue, which is how I like it.

I had just moved north of London at the time, which was great because Sara lived close by, and when I met Craig at a weekend seminar at Eastbourne, he told me he was having problems finding a good private circle where he lived and asked whether I knew any mediums who could help him. I asked where he lived, and lo and behold, we were practically neighbours. More than this, it was confirmation for me because I had been told by spirit that two people, one young and one old (sorry, Colin), were on their way.

Craig was 31 and was, I suppose, at the start of his journey in spiritual matters. He was a much more outgoing guy than Steven had been when I first met him and he had a real thirst for knowledge. The cycle of teaching a student was coming round again for me, but I knew Craig was right for the circle.

As for Colin – well, he is someone who has brought experience to our group. He has been a working medium for years, and is very well read and well practised in all that we are trying to teach. I had come across him several times before at seminars in Eastbourne and it turned out that he and Sara already knew each other too. They had met at a spiritual seminar in the Arthur Findlay College at Stansted Hall in Essex. This is a place where people can take courses in psychic and spiritual studies. It is a small world as it is, but when you embark on your spiritual journey, it gets even smaller.

Our circle felt more complete now and it was good to bring in the new energy. Normally it takes a while for everyone to adjust, but I must admit that this circle seemed to flow from the start and that was felt by all of us. If our last circle was preparation for this one, then what would this one bring, I wondered.

Some of the sitters in the group were experiencing episodes like the one we had in Germany when Chi was able to guide Petra and her guide around a room. For Craig, the whole thing was completely new, but I understand why spirit wanted this element in the circle:

it is important to keep passing the teachings to the young. I recognized the same thing with Mrs Primrose – she never wanted to work only with seasoned mediums, but to share her knowledge with the young so as to invest in the future.

A lot of it is really about being able to detect atmosphere, and how it changes when new energies are added or taken away. Even in our homes and places of work we sense the atmosphere, and more often than not can tell immediately if there is a change.

In the circle, which becomes your spiritual classroom, your sixth sense becomes more apparent and you feel the essence of the empty space around you which normally goes completely unnoticed in everyday life, where we depend so much on our other five senses.

It is by expanding this inner sense that we can detect the spirits who are around us, and from this perspective everything seems different. We learn mindfulness, compassion and many other virtues because we have stopped leading our busy lives for long enough to realize that material things are not as important as we thought and that stresses and fears are usually connected to the more earthly needs and demands we have.

We use this space to listen to and understand each other and form a support group where we feel safe enough to open up about our faults and fears and know that we will not be judged. Our circle is a safe place, a place out of the everyday world where we can be comfortable in our own skin. But it goes beyond skin: this is where we share our most personal energy, the part of us that can cause us to love and be loved. We become a spiritual family in every sense of the words.

Master Chi

Chi made himself known to the new circle after about ten weeks of sitting. If we are a family, then he would definitely be head of the family. And with the compassion of a good father, he gently steers us, guiding and advising but never judging, through our lessons.

Speaking through me during a trance session, he talked about the circle and why it was important for us to learn about the life beyond the physical world:

Blessings to you.

It is a joy to come and meet some of you for the first time. It is important that you know that spirit is with you and wishes to connect with you to help you understand your nature and why you are where you are now, doing what you are in this group.

It is a force inside each of you that has brought you here. That force is as elemental a part of you as your body, the blood which flows through your veins or the air inside your lungs. It is your nature, and like all aspects of you, it has a purpose. The purpose of it is to direct you, to pull you towards your destiny and allow you to get to the place in this world at which you aimed your consciousness even before you arrived here.

Therefore I say to you that right now you are where you are supposed to be.

It is the nature of the human life to expand, as it is for the spirit life. That is one thing you remember from before you came. You remember it because it is part of your nature, you see.

Some men are born to expand their minds and create devices and machines which will improve the living qualities of people; others will create systems which can be used to be counted on to give structure and keep people in order as they progress. Many bring in their nature a key to expansion to keep the human world advancing, but you, you have brought in your nature a key to open a door between worlds.

The little space you occupy as a group is seen as a light from the spirit world; it flashes from the dark density of the human world and reminds us that we are part of you and that you need us to bring light into the darkness. Like the flower calls to the bee to complete her, the bee knows that he must follow his nature. This is so for the spirit who hears the calling of the Earth spirit.

We are helping you to prepare your space so that we may co-mingle with you and assist you to understand more truths. But know that all is as it should be for now. You will have many questions, as do all children when a teacher enters the classroom. Let what you learn in the coming months be the contemplation you choose to pick questions from when we next share this space.

Blessings to you.

Over the years my guide has given many teachings to the groups I have sat in. It was good to hear from him in our new circle. He hadn't come through so much at the end of the old circle because he told us that when we were doing things properly, he would not have to come. But now he obviously wanted to come and introduce himself to the new group and inform us that he was watching over us and would come at times to help clear any confusion about the working of the circle.

Master Chi has also, on rare occasions, spoken through me in trance when I have been part of a spiritual seminar or Spiritualist teaching course. On one such course at the Arthur Findlay College, several of the mediums were asked to demonstrate trance for the students and I was one of those they asked. I must say that I cannot expect my guide to come and speak just because people ask me to. However, I always believe that Chi, or other spirit people he might wish to bring through, will come when they have a good reason to.

That particular day I went into the silence in front of a couple of hundred people crowded into one of the rooms in the college. It was open week and hundreds of people turned up because it was a trance day. I asked my guide if he would come, welcomed him into my space and hoped for the best, really.

Chi came through and spoke in his very gentle, sometimes witty manner. I, as always, was slightly aware of what was going on, but my mind wasn't involved and I enjoyed the peaceful state I found myself in. It took me a moment to even care that my body was moving: my guide was walking me into the body of the crowd.

A woman sitting quite far back was asking about her daughter in the spirit world. Chi walked me to her, gave her a very special evidential message straight from her child and then walked me backwards onto the platform. That was fine – I never even considered that my body might knock into someone or something. That is the level of trust I expect my sitters to get to if they are to work in trance.

The Fifth Module

Steven and I were getting ready to fly off to Frankfurt for the last of our five modules. It had been just short of a year since we started and now we were going to put the students through their paces and let them show us the results of all their hard work. We were both very excited and looking forward to seeing them all again. Even though the course was just five weekends out of a full year, there was a thread of continuity running through it and we needed to follow it to the end. We had also become quite connected to the group and it was great to hear about their progression between modules. They loved their development and took all the things we asked them to do in their own circles so seriously. We couldn't have asked for more enthusiastic students.

On the first day we took the students through exercises from all the previous modules to see how far they had come. It was clear they had come quite a way from that first day! Monica, our translator, who had been with us all the way through, remarked to me how much she was aware of their progress, and she works on lots of spiritual seminars. It made me very happy to be there to watch the progress of these very dedicated students.

When we had them giving messages, all of them worked amazingly well and gave good information to one another. It was also excellent to hear them differentiate between mediumship and psychic information. One of the women, called Ute, who had been quite quiet and reserved throughout the course, ended up rather forcefully pontificating about the sections of the reading she had just given that went from a very strong spiritual link to more dense and heavy psychic information which took a lot out of her before she managed to re-establish her spirit link again.

Stephan, who had always been one to ask a lot of questions and who we had thought would be very doubtful about the mediumistic and psychic work, actually surprised us all because he gave a fantastic reading to his partner with complete self-assurance. He had always favoured the healing side of the work, but I think he finally got it that mediumship is a form of healing and that really worked for him.

The final session of the day was left to trance! Sorry. We put the students back into their four circles and I took them through the trance exercise and then left them to work in circle and let their spirit guides direct them. It was heavenly, to say the least. Monica said she would have loved to just let go and be with them, but of course she couldn't, such were the conditions in the room. We had only introduced them to trance work just over a month earlier, but they seemed to totally understand what was asked of them. For many years I have seen people come to trance groups and in no time become very deluded. This group was serious about development and remained very well grounded throughout the entire course.

Normally we would end the first day of a module with a question and answer session, but this time the students asked me to give a demonstration of trance and let them meet Chi.

Whenever I am asked to do this I take myself off somewhere quiet and ask Chi if he would like to work through me. I always feel that it is courteous to get permission from my guide, because at the end of the day I could sit in a trance state, but he might not come and speak. This time, though, I could already feel that the energies in the room were such that my guide would come.

Steven had met Chi several times by now and knew how to prepare people for what might happen when he came to speak. He began to talk to the group as I took myself off into the silence and prepared to link with spirit.

In just a few minutes I could feel the vibration around my body increase and a great surge of energy run through me as my guide came close to me. I could feel that he was adjusting his own much faster vibration to link with mine. At this point I felt the sensations I have become used to over the years as my mind drifts into a dreamlike state. My focus on the room I was in was fading away, but I felt so comfortable, as if I was wrapped in a warm bale of cotton wool.

Chi came through with his usual greeting and introduced himself to the students. Steven told me that the room fell into a deathly silence, as if Chi's presence had put them into a waking coma. He recorded the session, which was good because when the students finally realized that Chi had a personality and a sense of humour, they snapped awake again and asked many questions:

Q: May I ask where Gordon's mind is at the moment and whether he is aware of what's going on?

Chi: The medium's mind is where it always is, but it has been desensitized to his surroundings for the moment. He has an awareness of what is going on, but no connection to it. It's a bit like hearing voices in another room discussing something you have no interest in – it's just background noise to him.

Q: Have you always been Gordon's guide and did you know him in the spirit world before he was born?

Chi: Yes. I chose to guide the medium from before he was born until the time he reawakens in the spirit world. We have always been connected, we just didn't always know it, just as a baby can't really know its parents until it has the awareness to do so, but it knows that there are beings looking after it and helping it. This is so with the medium and me. The more we learn to trust our guardians, the more we can bond with them and grow.

Q: Can you explain the universe to us?

Chi: If I could, do you think you would be able to understand it? Just try to understand yourself more and learn from your life. Be as open and aware and truthful with yourself as you can be. The more you know about yourself, the smaller the universe will seem.

Q: What is it like when we die? I'm not afraid, but will we be alone at any time, or will there be family and friends waiting to meet us?

Chi: First I must say that it is like most things you don't know – when it happens, it's never as bad as you imagine. For you it will feel like a short sensation of acceleration and then release – release into a state of peace and weightlessness which you truly cannot imagine at this point, but those who are bonded and connected to you will be by your side even before the moment of liberation. The reason your loved ones attend is to adjust your vibration, much like I have done with the medium just now.

Q: Can you remember your life on Earth?

Chi: Yes, if I choose to, but try not to allow the past to become your master. Learn to be in control of the here and now.

Q: What will happen after 2012? I am very worried that there will be wars and disasters and that other terrible things will happen to our planet. Do you have any information that we might use to prepare ourselves?

Chi: Forgive my flippancy, but after 2012 will come 2013, if I'm not mistaken. Madame, if you look at the things which you fear in the future, you will see that they are all happening in your world today, but the planet keeps turning and sustaining life regardless. Like the gentleman I spoke to earlier, do not feel that you have to deal with the world's problems, but look more to bringing balance to yourself and those around you. And again, be in the now, as it is certain, but tomorrow is still in the making.

Q: Do you think that science will ever understand the spirit world and even find a way to communicate with it through machinery?

Chi: Strange that the greatest machine on Earth has already been able to communicate with the world of its ancestors for thousands of years and that man would try to build something inferior to the human body to do this, but I do understand your question, and as long as man looks to expand his knowledge in this world, at some point he will meet the higher power of spirit. Have you ever *considered that the spirit world needs to be separate from the mind of man? Remember, all men come from the spirit world and will return to it eventually and there you have no need of gadgets in order to communicate.*

Q: What is the one thing you could tell us that would help us to be more like spirit at a higher level and bring more light into our lives?

Chi: The simple answer is that you have to learn to love yourself and one another. This has been said so many times and must be said until the day comes when love is constant, but you are not spirit at a higher level when you walk the Earth, and nor should you be. You have chosen to come and learn from the restrictions and emotional episodes which the human existence will give you. And as for light, it is always there; only the shadows of a memory of darkness keep the light from your mind. But remember, the real light is there, always there inside you.

The students loved their session with Chi and he answered several other questions which were personal to them. One thing which was addressed to Steven at the end of the session was that he and I would get a great surprise the following day and we should welcome it with open arms. This brought forth lots of titters from the students, because unknown to us they had bought us both presents to thank us for the teaching.

The trance was a gift for the students themselves which they never expected. It was the end of all the lessons and exercises; the following day would be devoted to giving each of the 40 students the opportunity to display something which they got from the course in front of the rest of the group.

I think this was one of the loveliest endings to any course or training session I had given in my years as a medium. Watching the students one by one stand up and speak about their experiences, talking from the heart about how much they had grown, both in themselves and in spiritual understanding, was a joy to say the least.

Some gave messages to show they had the confidence to do so now. One of these was Thomas, and he did very well. He also thanked Steven for personally helping him to improve his link with his guide and expressed his appreciation of the acceptance he had been shown by all of the other students, even though he had doubted so much in the early modules.

But it was Lana who really inspired us when she confidently spoke for ten minutes about how much tougher she had become through the development and where she was going in her life. She explained that she had been so timid at the start that she had never had the confidence to speak to men or even let them come anywhere near her, but in the weeks leading up to the final module she had met someone and instead of shying away, she had opened up and seized the moment. Now she proudly announced that she was in love and part of a couple, and she beamed with joy.

I could give example after example, but overall it was a great success for us and the students and we all felt it and shared our gratitude with one another.

Steven and I did get a beautiful gift each from the students, but I wasn't sure that this was what Chi had meant by a surprise. Somehow I felt there was still something left to happen that day.

The Final Surprise

It was over, the first of our courses of intuitive studies had come to an end, and all that was left to do now was to go home. Steven and I headed for the airport again. It was so familiar by now.

We were both still reeling from the very high energy of the past two days when suddenly I had a strange feeling run through me. It was a good feeling, the kind of feeling I would get when I was a child and I knew that something good was going to happen just before it did.

Steven, like me, had been a very sensitive child. Now he looked at me and said that he had a strange feeling, but he didn't understand it. I told him I felt the same. We both assumed it would be something to do with Chi's surprise. At the very same moment we said, 'Paul is going to be on our plane!' I think we were so sure that we might even have willed the guy from another city! It's hard to explain, but when you have a feeling like this it becomes so certain that I would bet my house on it if I were a gambling man.

We had been in and out of this airport so much and we had always thought we would meet Paul again, but we never had. This time we were both so sure, and as we boarded the plane, there he was.

It was great to see him again and to make sure this time that we got him to our circle. He was equally happy to see us and said that he had a funny feeling that he would run into us again.

It was the end of our teaching in Frankfurt, but we still had a circle to build and now we had found the person we needed to make it complete.

11

THE CIRCLE GOES FORWARD

Many people are drawn to the spiritual path in search of phenomena and metaphysical wonders. Yet the greatest phenomenon you can experience on the spiritual path is love. When you sit together in your group, sit as friends and love will appear.

MASTER CHI

Paul took to the circle so easily. He had only asked to come for one visit originally, but I think he knew after his first sitting that he would be invited back.

And so it was that our circle began to grow in energy and strength. Sara and Steven were soon able to let go enough to allow their spirit guides to link with them in trance and I would link with both at the same time and guide them to connect with each other. Part of this process involved making them touch the very tips of their fingers together and have one of them move their hands very quickly whilst guiding the other to follow. We have all tried to replicate this exercise with our eyes open, out of trance, and it can't be done. Well, certainly not with the same fluidity as when spirit does it when we are in trance. This shows that if you let go, spirit will be there. It has also allowed us to feel the strength of our spirit guides and how aware they are, much more so than we can ever be.

Even in the early stages of the circle I felt that we were making a stronger link with spirit for a reason. Spirit is preparing something and I bet it is being sensed by others who are sitting in private circles at this time. Sandra and Christine, who sat with us for years, still keep a circle going and it's amazing that whenever we get an indication that spirit is doing something different, you can be sure that one of them will call with the same thing.

Since we now had all the right people for the group, Chi came on several occasions to give instructions to us. On his first visit after Paul had joined us he spoke to everyone and as always thanked them for allowing him to be present. Then he gave a short explanation of what was happening from the spirit side when they prepared the circle:

> *Spirit is preparing this space as you know to allow the teachings and essence of the higher mind to filter into your world. It is clear that each of you already knows that this is not about the individual, but the unit. The strength you will gain from giving yourselves to the unit will be more than you can imagine in this life. There will still have to be much breaking down of the individual ego, but this will happen as we progress with our mission.*

When you come to the circle, you must first learn to be relaxed with one another; this is so important for your progression and for the strength of the unit. It will always be clear if there are differences between you. It will be felt by all; there is no place in a circle like this to hide your feelings. Part of why you are here is to recognize your feelings, understand your fears and accept that you are not perfect in the human state. Spirit will guide you in a way which is sure and steady and will only ever allow you to deal with what you are ready for; it is never the way of spirit to force or rush, only to gently flow.

Some of you have been on the path longer than others and have opened doors with your persistence and effort which have allowed all of you to be sitting here now. This is as it should be, as teaching of any kind must pass from the experienced to the inexperienced in order for it to mean anything.

You will find that this particular circle has all the ingredients required to produce a new phenomenon, one which we have been preparing for your world for some time now and which will need to be broken down in stages.

Don't be alarmed if you become aware of certain states you find yourself in during your sitting that at first you cannot process through your thinking mind. This is part of what you have to come through with us to truly experience our world as never before.

The phenomena of the past are not what we are looking to achieve with this circle. No, these are laughed at in these modern times and would not marry well with the way the human mind is evolving today. All I can ask of you at this time is this: be open and harmonious with one another, allow friendships to develop between you, and when you open your sacred space to spirit, trust with all your heart that each new experience is preparation for lifting you to the higher mind for the sake of spiritual advancement.

Blessings to you.

Chi must have sensed that everyone had questions about what was coming, but true to his nature he left us with the most infuriating statement any spiritual teacher can leave students with: *'No questions tonight, my friends, but trust me, all will become clear in time.'*

The words Chi gave us that night made us all consider what the spirit world had in mind for the new circle.

Already we were experiencing much deeper sessions than ever before. I had had glimpses of a kind of trance where my mind went completely out of it for a short period of time and the whole circle, even the new sitters like Paul and Craig, were being taken to levels of trance that you felt would normally have taken years to achieve. When Chi came to speak at the end of a session, it felt as though I had to be brought gradually back to the state of mind I once thought was deep. Now that seemed very light and more like an overshadowing than a trance.

It always seemed that I had to experience this type of inner journey several weeks before the other sitters. I sometimes felt like an explorer who had been sent out from the camp to scout around and see what lay ahead. Each time this happened I found that my awareness was becoming clearer in the depth of the experience – like going into a very dark empty space and having to give your sight time to adjust.

When this happened I didn't share it with the circle right away because I didn't want to put ideas in their heads. I knew that very soon I would hear from all of them that they had just come through a type of episode which I had gone through myself several weeks earlier.

Also, the energy in the circle had become so dense that everybody was mentioning that the spirits who came into the circle were solid. All of us had felt hands touch us or a solid person brush against us during the circle. It felt as though we were creating such a density of energy that the spirits were able to present themselves as though we were in the same reality as they were. Again, I had had glimpses of this over the years, but it was becoming much more defined.

The other incredible thing that happened was that Chi would come and talk on a subject that one of the circle members had been discussing earlier and would give an opinion on what was said. In this way he let us know that our guides were listening to us and were very aware of where our minds were, even when we were not in circle. As a medium I had known this for years, but it was nice to get the confirmation. And it was so good for the new sitters to experience this.

Colin, for example, had been watching a documentary on a philosopher who had been discussing freedom, and later he talked it over with some friends. At the end of our circle that week, Chi came through and told Colin that he had been listening to the conversation and wished to add something for us to ponder on:

Blessing to you, my friends.

I could not help but connect to your discussion earlier about freedom. So many words seemed to contaminate the purity of the word itself. Remember, you have come from a state of freedom in the spirit world and it was your choice to come to a word of confinement and restriction in this physical realm.

In your discussion there was talk of fighting for freedom, yet fights in the physical world restrict your freedom more often than allow it to be.

All of the things you find restricting in this world are the result of fear and human desire. Need can blind and confine you, and in confinement your nature will cause you to struggle.

So, be still, relax and realize that it is your destiny to return to the freedom from which you came. The body will die, and with it the struggle if you strive to be calm in your lifetime here.

Free yourself now by remembering who you are: you are spirit and as such you are always free. By preparing the mind and setting it to a higher tone whilst in the body, you can break some of the ties which hold you to the earthly existence with all of its fears and thoughts of desire.

Don't allow the thinking mind to become your gaoler; freedom is a state of grace and lives only in the heart of self.

The times when spirits have come to us and given us information which shows that they are connected to us and part of our everyday lives is very reassuring. It is the same when they make correct predictions. This tells us that we are dealing with a very intelligent source which has the perspective to see beyond what we see and know.

It has never been a part of my thinking to use that source for anything other than spiritual progression. The spirit world should never be seen as a service which can solve all our earthly problems and heal every hurt we must endure in this human lifetime. Remember what Chi said: they are always there to gently guide and steer us, but we ourselves have a duty to expand our minds and evolve in a spiritual way. They can help us, but mostly they try to help those who wish to help themselves.

I look at Steven and see how his own thinking has evolved since being part of the circle. He has made a very strong connection to his guides and as a result will very rarely ask for help from me or Jim now. Most recently, when we gave a joint demonstration of mediumship in Sweden, rather than ask me to help him or give him words of advice before he went onto the platform, he sat on his own and asked his guide, Chen Tsung, how he could give clear messages from the spirit world that night. This is what he got:

As I sat to tune in to my guide, my mind became clear and then I felt his familiar presence. I heard his words coming through my mind in response to the question I had just asked him:

'Imagine pure clear water running through the gutter of a building, flowing clearly towards the pipe which will bring it down to the ground. The flow will become impeded if there has been a build-up of debris such as leaves and stones over the years; if this is the case, then there will be a blockage and the flow will slow and no more than a few drops of water will pass through the pipe.

'In relationship to your work, see the spirit message as the water which has to flow clearly, your mind as the pipe through which it has to flow and the debris as your emotions, fears and doubts which may have gathered over the years.

'As you have developed, you have removed much of the emotional debris from your mind,

*so have no fear that the spirit message will
have a clear channel to pass through.'*

This is a lovely simple message for any fledgling medium to contemplate before they work for spirit. Incidentally, Steven gave very accurate and comforting messages that night. I believe that even the response he heard when asking the question allowed him to realize that his guide was there and ready to work, and his request for help was more for the people who needed a message from a loved one than for himself. This again shows how spirit responds to us when the help we ask for is not for ourselves but for those in greater need. It's this thinking that makes our circle work.

The circle you create must be like a close family, with strong bonds and openness to one another's weaknesses and strengths; acceptance and appreciation of both are vital. The trust you build with the spirit world will depend on how your attitude has been shaped by your life experiences. Most likely the tougher ones will be your greatest teachings. But it is your determination to attend, come hell or high water, that will be the making of you in any circle and will add strength to the energy in the group.

The success of so many of the old Spiritualist circles was as much down to the dedication and devotion of the people who attended them as to the spirits who appeared in them. There is not one person in my circle who would rather be anywhere else on circle night. This is something I have tried for years to get through to people who come into spiritual development: what you put into it will determine what you get out of it.

Lessons from Spirit

All questions have answers. Why is this so?
It is because there is an answer that the question arises.
Answers are neither mysteries nor profound, they are
quite simply understandings waiting to be realized.

MASTER CHI

It is such a good feeling to be part of a circle and feel the link between each sitter, knowing that higher-minded beings have orchestrated this and brought us all together. Just the thought of how connected we all are and that there is a bigger force in the universe that guides us always makes me feel contented. And the many lessons we receive from the spirit world make us feel as though we have taken a course in the University of Life.

When Chi spoke to us about freedom, he mentioned that we all come from the spirit world and will all eventually return to that higher state at some point. This opened up many questions in my mind and in the mind of others in the circle that led us into a deep discussion, which is, I'm sure, exactly what my guide wanted. It is the way of spirit to filter things down through our minds so that we expand on them and try to understand life at a much deeper level.

Whenever a great spiritual mind has come into any of the circles I have been in, a certain feeling has filled the room. It's not just what they say that lets you know that you are in the presence of a very evolved spiritual being, it's the essence in the room and how the words they choose to speak affect each sitter in a very personal way, leaving them feeling that they have just had a personal conversation with a master.

Most of the encounters with guides and teachers from the other side have taken place in private circles and with groups of close friends. This means that most of that wisdom will never be shared or passed on to others. The effect of the teaching Chi gave to the German students made me think that there was now a need to let some of those words go out to as many people as possible.

Here is just a selection from the question and answer sessions we have had over the years in the two private circles I have sat in when Chi or another teacher has come through. These are the types of question people in development might ask a spirit teacher if given the chance:

Q: Do you have a body of any kind?

A: There is a vehicle of sorts, but not in the form that you would call a body. This is only required when descending into realms where identity is important. The more you evolve, the less of you is required.

Q: Why then do mediums see spirits as they looked when they were human? And why, when people die and say they have met their family and other people they knew who died before them, do they always mention bodies?

A: In this case I must say that it is the medium who has to have something to describe to a relative, so the spirit being will project an image of what they looked like to the mind of the medium so that they can be recognized by their loved one. And in the case of people returning to the spirit world, again it is they who need to see the familiarity of the body of their relatives. But even that spirit who has just passed no longer has a body, they just haven't realized it yet. Maybe now you will understand some of the power of your mind – it can create that which is not there. This is why in your development we give so many lessons about the mind: so that you can learn to think like spirit before you eventually leave the physical world.

Q: Why don't God or the spirit world intervene at times and stop some of the horrible tragedies in our world? Why do they let people suffer?

A: The human world is a world where pain and suffering are experienced and there are times when spirit would like to take away the suffering, but that would mean there would be no need for a physical existence. Imagine for a moment that your daughters just arrived in your life at the age of 20: you would not have nursed them through some of the most important times of their lives, times which caused you to bond with them emotionally and feel love for them. This is what it would feel like in the spirit world if we were to erase some of the suffering in your world; if we acknowledge the love which comes from suffering, then pain is never seen as a punishment.

Q: Why can't I see spirit people or hear them like other mediums say they can? I do feel the presence of spirits around me, but apart from asking them to let me see or hear them, what can I do to improve my gift?

*A: Seeing and hearing are two of the human senses; the part of you that can develop more is the part that **feels** the presence of spirits. When you are ready to understand the language of spirit you will know the answers through what you feel. You would add nothing to your gift if we just made it easy for you, and you would not grow as a conscious being. Neither look for spirits with your eyes, nor listen with your ears, but sense and feel them in your heart.*

Q: Do I have anything to be afraid of when I am in circle and opening up to the unseen world?

A: You have absolutely nothing to fear from spirit. The only thing you can fear is fear itself. The world of spirit is not to be found in the shadows of the human mind but in the light. In order to understand it you have to travel through your own mind, recognizing where your fear lies. In so doing you will see that you too are spirit and that simple recognition will bring light back to you and dispel all the shadows from your mind and fear will be no more. So remember, the real you, the spirit you, is where we are trying to guide you to.

Q: I have heard it said that we go through a tunnel when we pass and that there is a sense of travel at high speed. Is this true?

A: It may seem like that to the mind which has come from the physical world, but it is more to do with vibration and frequency than structures and travel. The body which you occupy uses space, time and distance in order to perceive reality. The spirit body, when released from the physical world, vibrates much more quickly than anything you will ever have sensed in your human life, and the conscious mind which creates your reality has to find perspective, so the heightened vibration will seem like speed and the tunnel will appear because the mind is no longer seeing through the eyes and automatically remembers the only other similar sensation it has encountered, which was coming through a birth tunnel from one world to the other. All of this will dissolve when the new frequency is set and the spirit begins to accept its new reality.

Q: What does the spirit world think about the human world just now and does it see how the future will be?

A: The spirit concept of the human world is that it is where it should be right now. To understand the future of human existence one needs to look at the entire human population as one being. That being has evolved like a newborn child and might be seen to be in its adolescent stage just now, as it is going through many changes and struggling to find its true identity. At this time there is as much unrest in the human mind as there would be in that of a teenager. There is rebellion against higher authorities and great misunderstandings about religious and spiritual truths. But you only have to observe its determination to progress and will to become greater and you will see that with the right parenting, it could reach adulthood.

The Best is Yet to Come...

I have hundreds of transcripts and recordings of spirit teachings over the years. Only now, in my new circle, have I even bothered to revisit some of the very wise words, predictions and insights I have heard. I know that my work is changing; recently, I read a transcript from 1999 and found that Dominica, one of my spiritual teachers of that time, had predicted that in ten years I would be preparing a new group of people for very important spiritual work which would lift people's minds to a much more spiritual level and would involve our circle experiencing spirit as never before. 'And,' she said, 'one you believe to have gone will come back into your life and help guide you from afar.'

How amazing that this was given way back then and is all happening now. Our current circle was started in 2009, ten years after the message was given, and we have all already had experiences we have never known before.

For a while I was puzzled by the one who would come back to guide from afar, but the teacher who had given those words had never been wrong, even with some of her more obscure prophecies. And it wasn't long before it came to pass.

The last circle we had at the end of the year, three days before Christmas, seemed to take us very deep again. Only Jim, Steve and I sitting that night, but the energy in the room was still very powerful. I remember feeling as if I was leaving my body. I could see the room, but from somewhere above where I was actually sitting, and it was as though I was looking down through a yellowish mist of some kind.

I noticed that someone was standing there with his arms folded in front of his body. He definitely looked like a Native American, but nevertheless I recognized him: he was Laura's guide. Laura was the most amazing trance medium I had ever witnessed in my life, and I knew that she had had out-of-body experiences since she was a child. In the time I knew her, she would call me and tell me things I had been doing five minutes earlier, right down to the last detail, because she had seen me doing them when she was having one of her out-of-body experiences.

Her guide was just standing there, but there was definitely a strong pulse coming from his direction. Then, in a moment he was gone and I felt as if I had been pulled back into my body at a rate of knots. The others were looking at me as if I had just appeared out of thin air and there was a feeling that something very powerful had happened, but no one seemed to have a clue what it was.

Jim asked me if I had been aware of anyone standing in the room – had I sensed a spirit presence that was unfamiliar to our circle? I told him I had and asked if he had seen them too. 'No,' he said, 'but I felt Laura standing in the corner.' Steven then said that he had seen a lady in the same place and described Laura to a tee. I told them both that I had not seen Laura herself but had seen her guide.

The last time I had seen Laura in the flesh had been 17 years earlier, when Mrs Primrose had died, and I hadn't had any contact with her at all in that time. On a couple of occasions I had been told by a mutual friend that she had cancer and was very ill, but since I had left Scotland I lost contact with that friend and had never heard any more about Laura. I honestly hadn't thought about her in years.

Our first feeling was that Laura must have passed to the spirit world and this was her way of letting us know. Also, she had almost died several times in her life and would find that out-of-body experiences would happen at these times.

The whole experience left Jim and me feeling very weird, to say the least. Steven wondered why we were feeling strange when we believed that when we go to the spirit world we are better off, but it wasn't this that left me cold, it was more to do with the depth of the out-of-body state I myself had experienced that night. There had been moments when I had actually felt that I was in the spirit world myself.

I looked through old diaries to find a number for the friend who knew Laura, but couldn't locate it.

The following evening, the night before Christmas Eve, Jim and I were sitting talking about the circle when my phone rang. For a second I felt my heart stop as if it was going to be bad news and Jim looked at me as if he was aware of what I was feeling. I looked at the number displayed and didn't recognize it, but I answered it anyway. I swear I could have died when I heard a woman's voice softly say my name: it was Laura.

If I was blown away by that, I was about to hear something much more shocking. After explaining how hard it had been to get in touch with me, she told me that I had to be the worst telepath she had ever worked with.

'Why?' I asked.

Laura explained that she had been coming to our circle for a while, but no one had noticed her. 'That boy Steven who sits with you,' she said, 'I walked right over to him last night and thought, "Are *none* of these people receptive to spirit?"'

'How do you know his name?' I asked her.

'Eventually,' she went on, totally ignoring me, 'I had to bring my guide with me to see if he could get your attention.'

She said she had been coming to the circle because spirit wanted me to experience something completely different, which hadn't been done before, and she was to watch over things.

You have no idea how this made me feel. I have witnessed spiritual episodes that most people will never believe and experienced mind-blowing phenomena which are out of this world, but this!

I told her we had picked up on her and her guide, but thought she was dead.

'Nearly,' she laughed, 'many times, but I still have things to do here, and getting you sorted out and in the right place to make this new connection with spirit is my priority.'

She went on to describe to me places I had been, people I had met and many, many, private episodes of my life in the recent past which there is no way anyone could have known unless they had been a fly on the wall. I was amazed. But, as she said, her main reason to get back in touch with me that night wasn't just to amaze me but to reconnect with Jim and me in preparation for the new work.

Now I knew the reason why, whenever I sat in the new circle, I became so quiet inside and felt that I was going deeper into trance than ever before. But what did it all mean? What kind of work did the spirit world have in mind, and why now and why me?

But what do you know? When I asked Laura, in the true form of a great spiritual teacher she simply replied, 'All will become clear in time...'

LIST OF EXERCISES

ABOUT THE AUTHOR

Hailed as 'the UK's best medium', **Gordon Smith** is renowned for his astonishing ability to pinpoint exact names of people, places and even streets relevant to a person's life.

From early childhood, Gordon had the ability to see, sense and hear spirit people. At the age of 24, he embarked on 15 years of study and practice, going on to develop his abilities as a medium – or messenger from the spirit world – under the tutelage of some of the great legends of the spiritualist church. Gordon is now a bestselling author and one of the world's top psychic mediums and spiritual teachers, conducting mediumship workshops and events around the world. His Celtic charm and lively demonstrations – delivered in his trademark style combining humour, pure passion, and empathy towards others – provide his audiences with a rare opportunity to experience the fascinating phenomenon of mediumship.

www.gordonsmithmedium.com
www.psychicviews.co.uk

Steven Levett entered the world of mediumship some 10 years ago, and his journey from ordinary south London guy to spiritual healer and medium has taken him through many classes, lessons and experiences that he could never have envisaged at the outset.

Steven now works as a medium and healer in the UK and abroad. He developed his gift with Gordon Smith, and together they now teach seminars and workshops to students all over Europe.

HAY HOUSE

Look within

Join the conversation about latest products, events, exclusive offers and more.

 Hay House UK

 @HayHouseUK

 @hayhouseuk

 healyourlife.com

We'd love to hear from you!